LEARNING

from GOD'S

IMPERFECT PEOPLE

ELMER TOWNS

DESTINY IMAGE® PUBLISHERS, INC.
P.O. Box 310, Shippensburg, PA 17257-0310
"Promoting Inspired Lives."

This book and all other Destiny Image and Destiny Image Fiction books are available at Christian bookstores and distributors worldwide.

For more information on foreign distributors, call 717-532-3040.

Reach us on the Internet: www.destinyimage.com.

ISBN 13 TP: 978-0-7684-8297-3

ISBN 13 eBook: 978-0-7684-8298-0

For Worldwide Distribution.

1 2 3 4 5 6 7 8 / 28 27 26 25 24

TABLE OF CONTENTS

PART THREE

PART FOUR

PART FIVE

Preface

PERFECT LESSONS FROM IMPERFECT PEOPLE

WHAT can you learn from imperfect people? They have many positive and negative lessons to teach you - you must know where, when, and how to look for them, but most importantly, how to apply them. Their strengths and weaknesses are focused on in this book.

Don't be impressed by your first glance at their strength. You probably already know what makes them tick and what makes them run. Their strengths are good lessons to learn, but what about their imperfections? What can their weaknesses teach you. Can you learn how they overcame their imperfections?

First learn from negative lessons, what not to do. You can see what they did wrong, or what they didn't do; you learn the consequences. But your life will not thrive just learning from negative consequences, i.e., learning what not to be.

Focus your life on the things God did for them, and seek to experience God's power and victory. Let these positive lessons change your life. Work for things you can do, or things you should do, or things God wants you to do. This is where imperfect people can give you suggestions that will transform your life. This way, you learn positive lessons from imperfect people: in spite of their ignorance, God led them to make "correct" decisions.

WHY GOD USES IMPERFECT PEOPLE

For His glory. If God used perfect people to preach a perfect sermon in a perfect way, people would glorify the preacher and his ability instead of God who works in hearts. When God uses any perfect workmen to do His work, people normally glorify the perfect workman, not God. Here is the ultimate goal for our life and ministry: "Now all glory to God who is able to make you strong" (Romans 16:25, NLT). God uses imperfect people so that all glory goes to Him.

As a testimony to the unsaved. Sometimes when a preacher is poorly equipped or stumbles over his words and shows other incompetence, then when God works through His Words to convict people of sin and transform their life into the image of Jesus Christ, that powerful ministry reflects on glory to God. Therefore, God uses imperfect people as a testimony to unsaved people so they will know that ultimate results are from God, not from the preacher.

"Remember...few of you were wise in the world's eyes...or powerful...or wealthy...instead God chose things that the world considers foolish...considered weak...considered despised...to bring to nothing what the world considers important...so no one can ever boast in the presence of God" (1 Corinthians 1:26-29, NLT).

To demonstrate the power of God. If a preacher is convincing, he may get credit for what is accomplished by his sermon. If a teacher is wise, he may get credit for what the students learn. If a counselor effectively gives good answers, she may get credit for the good direction she gives. But when God uses an imperfect person, He demonstrates, "The message of the cross...is the very power of God" (1 Corinthians 1:18).

WHY GOD USES IMPERFECT PEOPLE

- So people will see God, not man
- So people will worship God unreservedly
- So people will be motivatived to service
- So the body of Christ will work together
- Because God's strategy is using imperfect people

WHAT IS GOD'S PRINCIPLE?

If there is any secret to the mystery of God's imperfect people, it is that fact that they recognize their weakness and let Christ work through them. All imperfect people must let Christ shine through their weaknesses so Christ can minister through and beyond it. "My old self has been crucified with Christ. It is no longer I who live, but Christ lives in me. So I live in this earthly body by trusting in the Son of God, who loved me and gave himself for me" (Galatians 2:20, NLT).

So God's work is not done in a worldly way. Don't expect the work of the church to be successful because it follows the principles of Wall Street, i.e., getting wealthy and successful through stocks and bonds, etc. Again the church should not follow the principles of successful sports, i.e., power, strategy and physical fitness; hoping to win the next encounter. You don't see influence of university learned wisdom building powerful life-transforming ministries. "You don't see among yourselves many of the wise... many of the ruling class...many of the nobles ... who are called" (1 Corinthians 1:26, J.B.Phillips New Testament). We must let Jesus minister through us because we are imperfect people. He wants to use imperfect people so the glory goes to God the Father and not to us.

As a result, God works through you. The secret of Christian ministry is not what you do for the church, but what you let Christ do through you. "My strength (Christ) is made perfect in weakness" (2 Corinthians 12:9).

To manifest God's power. When God uses imperfect people, He manifests His power through them to accomplish the task. "My (Christ) power works best through weak people" (2 Corinthians 12:9, TLB).

Because God calls a man/woman and does His work through them. So, look again at the Book of Judges—both male and female judges—each won a victory over their enemies. But look again at the list of the weaknesses of each judge. It was the power of God working unmistakably through them so that God got the glory. "The Lord raised up a rescuer to save them" (Judges 3:9 NLT).

The ultimate purpose is to glorify God. The Bible teaches, "God had chosen the weak things" (see 1 Corinthians 1:28). The Bible could have just as easily said, "God had chosen the imperfect things." Why? "That no one can ever boast in the presence of God" (1 Corinthians 1:29, NLT).

But if you are imperfect, don't stay that way, strive for perfection, i.e., to do the best you can. How can you be more perfect? By getting a vision of what God can do through you and more importantly what God can do with you. You have gifts and talents, make sure God works through them to accomplish His ministry.

Second, find God's plan for your life, and let that plan be fulfilled through you. "'For I know the plans I have for you,' says the Lord. 'They are plans for good and not for disaster, to give you a future and a hope'" (Jeremiah 29:11, NLT).

Third, don't stay focused on your weaknesses—let them guide you to live in the power of Christ. Let your weaknesses be the foundation on which you build your talents through the power of Christ. Remember weaknesses are weaknesses, they are not the defining statement of your life—Christ is. Always be aware of your weakness, but focus on your strength in Christ. Let your strengths guide your life. Use your strengths to overcome and strengthen your ministry.

In the early days of Liberty University, David Rhodenhizer, one of the universities first freshmen, had graduated from high school with a terrible speech impediment—he stuttered. When I met him, I thought he could never be a preacher—maybe a good administrator in a church, but not a preacher. Because of his physical limitation, he was sent to a special state-supported rehab program to learn how to speak clearly and distinctly. It did not help as much as prayer and godly direction.

Mr. Worley, a deacon at Thomas Road Baptist Church, took David under his wing, asking him to help teach his junior boys Sunday school class. Worley did most of the teaching, but every once in a while asked David to step in to tell a story or explain a verse. David had time to think what he was going to say, plan it, and spoke clearly and distinctly without stuttering. Over a period of time, David was able to speak clearly. Eventually he was able to teach the whole lesson without the help of Worley.

Today, David Rhodenhizer is approximately 70 years old and pastors Calvary Road Baptist Church in Northern Virginia. He planted the church in the 1970s and built the attendance to over 1,000. He has planted other satellite churches in Washington, DC.

Work from your strengths that will lift your weaknesses. Your strength is always in Jesus Christ. Remember, Paul said, "I can do all things through Christ who strengthens me" (Philippians 4:13).

DICTIONARY DEFINITION OF IMPERFECT

Imperfect: /imˈpərfəkt/ (1) characterized by, or subject to defects, (2) not perfect, (3) lacking completeness, (4) lacking certain parts, (5) denoting actions or state still in process, (6) at a point not perfect, (7) not what it was, or is going to be compared to past, or to future, (8) unfinished.

Synonym: incomplete, rudiment, undeveloped, defective in some point or part, still developing, embryonic, arrested development.

YOUR IMPERFECTION

All of God's people are imperfect, and some are more imperfect than others. And those who are better than the average are still imperfect. God had no choice but to work with imperfect people. Since none are prefect, He sent His Son Jesus Christ to live a perfect life—as our example—then Jesus died for your imperfections (sins). That way, God can forgive imperfect people to prepare them for Heaven.

The greatest gift is the perfect record of Jesus - the Father accounts this to you so that when He looks at you, he sees the perfection of Jesus Christ. This perfection comes from your heavenly position, not your earthly life.

On earth, God gave you the Scriptures which teaches us the standard by which we should live. And His Words, (in the Bible) are embedded with His life and energy to help transform you to live by God's expectations.

The Father sent the Holy Spirit to regenerate you at salvation with new life. Now the Spirit lives in you, encouraging you, guiding you, and teaching you—all to lift your imperfections up to the Father's standard of holiness and righteousness.

Everything in your Christian life begins with your imperfect life, but God never leaves you in that condition. God wants you to enjoy the perfection you have in Jesus Christ, then live a new transformed life that demonstrates the power of His expectation.

MY PRAYER

Thank You Lord for loving me in spite of my imperfections, for saving me and filling me with the indwelling of Jesus Christ who enables me to live by faith and testify of Your goodness and power.

Overview

WHAT THIS BOOK
IS ALL ABOUT

P ERFECT people are not real, and real people are not perfect. One thing we know about human nature is that humans want to do right, but they don't always do right—eventually they will do wrong. Human nature wants to tell the truth, but sometimes humans find it necessary to fudge a little or tell a "white lie." Because imperfect people have a sinful nature, they are attracted to satan and his lies and fall prey to sin. The only perfect person is Jesus Christ, and His perfection was made immortal by His crucifixion.

We will never find a perfect person as our example. Everyone knows they are not perfect; as a result, everyone knows there is no one else who is perfect. Again, the only perfect person is Jesus Christ.

While we cannot be perfect, we can be inspired by other imperfect people, especially when they use their imperfection as a means to win a victory or to please God in their worship or service.

If God used only perfect people, He could not get anything done in this life. Why? Because no one would be used by Him, because no one qualifies—we are all imperfect.

It would be hard to live with a perfect person on this earth, especially if they demand that we be as perfect as they are. In essence, we could not live with a perfect human, because we would never measure up.

You can love yourself even if you are not a perfect person, and you can love another even when they are not perfect. Loving others begins by accepting an imperfect person, and their acceptance of you, all the while remembering both of you are imperfect.

And what is love? Love is the giving of yourself to another. Didn't Jesus say, "Greater love has no one than this, that a man gives his life for the one he loves" (John 15:13, ELT). The apostle John explained love with this definition, "Here is love, not that we love God, but that God loved us and gave His Son to die for our sins" (1 John 4:10, ELT).

LEARNING FROM IMPERFECT PEOPLE

Therefore, how can you, an imperfect person, love another person? You start with change—change your life to be the life you wish to see in the other person.

In other words, one person—you—can make a difference in other people by loving them and then receiving the love they offer you. When everyone tries to love another person—and we all do it together—love can change the world.

LEARNING FROM IMPERFECT JACOB

Jacob was the grandson of Abraham, the father of the Hebrews, God's people. God had promised that through Abraham's children He would bless the world. But imperfect Jacob was anything but a role model. If anything, at the beginning of his life, imperfect Jacob was usually acting imperfectly. How did God transform Jacob into becoming a person who could be used to bless the world?

God used a dream.

Imperfect Jacob had cheated his brother Esau out of the family birthright and inheritance. Imperfect Esau threatened to kill Jacob. So Jacob left his father's home to begin walking on an 800 mile trip to Tigris Euphrates Valley where he would meet his relative, Laban. There he would ultimately marry his daughters, Leah and Rebekah. That first night from home, Jacob's life was changed by a dream.

Jacob saw a ladder in his dream reaching up to heaven. But it was not the ladder that was important, "At the top of the stairway stood the Lord and He said, 'I am the Lord, the God of your grandfather Abraham, the God of your father Isaac'" (Genesis

28:13, NLT). Seeing God in a dream changed Jacob's life direction and ultimately made him a man of God. Could God change your life with a dream?

What did God tell Jacob that changed his life? "At the top of the stairway stood the Lord, who said, 'The ground you are lying on belongs to you. I am giving it to you and your descendants. Your descendants will be as numerous as the dust of the earth! They will spread out in all directions—to the west and the east, to the north and the south. And all the families of the earth will be blessed through you and your descendants. What's more, I am with you, and I will protect you wherever you go. One day I will bring you back to this land. I will not leave you until I have finished giving you everything I have promised you'"(Genesis 28:13-15, NLT). Wow—what a dream—the land he didn't own would one day belong to his family. His family would bless all people on the earth. And God promised to be with him, protect him, and guide him.

What can we learn from Jacob? *A dream from God can motivate imperfect Jacob as well as you, to live through many difficulties, failures, and imperfections to reach God's plan for your life.*

NOAH—IMPERFECT IN OLD AGE

Noah was not originally called an imperfect person, but rather "Noah was a righteous man, the only blameless person living on earth at the time, and he walked in close fellowship with God" (Genesis 6:9, NLT). The Bible does not say that Noah was a perfect person. NO! The Bible calls him righteous. The Scriptures reveal God doesn't make you righteous, rather He *declares* you will be righteous when He looks at your sin and forgives you through the cross of Jesus Christ. That means you are not made righteous. Noah obeyed God, he always did the right thing...until later in life. Then he became imperfect as an older man. He got drunk, and the consequences harmed his grandson.

What can we learn from the imperfections of Noah? *You can walk with God all your life and He can use you for great things, but in one foolish decision toward the end of your life, you can destroy your testimony and some of the lives that look up to you.*

PETER THE ROCK—WAS CHIPPED

Every time the New Testament lists the twelve apostles of Jesus Christ, Peter was always mentioned first. That is because he was the leader, many times he spoke for the group, and when Jesus wanted answers from the disciples, He usually directed His question to Peter. And on the day of Pentecost, God used Peter to preach a powerful sermon that was translated into many languages, so it could be understood by the crowd of Jews from all parts of the earth. Over 3,000 were saved and baptized that day.

The name Peter means rock, and many have likened him to a granite rock. But, on several occasions the granite rock was chipped. Peter took exception with Jesus and tried to correct Him. "But Peter took Him (Jesus) aside and reprimand Him" (Matthew 16:22, NLT). Just as quickly, "Jesus turned to Peter and said, 'Get away from me, satan! You are a dangerous trap to me. You are seeing things merely from a human point of view, not from God's'" (Matthew 16:23, NLT).

That event was not Peter's worst offense. On the night Jesus was betrayed and was being cross-examined by the high priest Caiaphas, Peter was outside the house warming himself with sinners by a fire. On three occasions a different person identified him as one of the disciples of Jesus. Twice he denied it, but on the third time, he not only denied, he cursed to make his point (Matthew 26:72). Because Peter

denied the Lord three times, when Jesus restored him back to fellowship, He asked Peter three times, "do you love Me?" (John 21:17). The obvious love of Jesus for one who denied Him indicates the forgiving heart of our Lord.

And what can we learn from an imperfect Peter? *You may have surrendered to God's call, and followed Jesus, but you can make a terrible decision against Him, like Peter did, but Jesus will love you, and He will restore you to useful ministry again if you let Him.*

GIDEON—GOD PUSHED A COWARD TO VICTORY

God used the imperfect Gideon to win a great battle. Gideon might have been the least likely to be called a man of God, and the least likely to be used greatly of God. Even Gideon gave the excuse, "My clan is the weakest in the whole tribe of Manasseh, and I am the least in my entire family!" (Judges 6:15). Even after God called Gideon, on several occasions Gideon gave excuses why he could not be used of God. Doesn't this qualify as imperfection?

God gave Gideon a great victory over 120,000 Midianties soldiers with only the help of 300 brave men. *The lesson—you may not be from the best family and you can be insecure...you may be timid...you may not be powerful, but when you answer God's call and obey His directions, He can use you to help win a great victory for His glory.*

THOMAS, A FOLLOWER OF JESUS, DOUBTED

Thomas was not the most prominent disciple following Jesus Christ; he was listed 8th on one occasion and 9th on another occasion. When he is first mentioned in Scripture, Thomas told Jesus why they should not go near Jerusalem where there was danger. Thomas used sarcasm when he said, "Let's go, too—and die with Jesus" (John 11:16, NLT). It is not surprising that Thomas was nicknamed, "doubting Thomas."

When Jesus was arrested in the Garden of Gethsemane, the eleven disciples all ran away to hide, but Thomas seemed to have run farther, and hid deeper than the other ten disciples. On Easter Sunday evening in the Upper Room, there were only 10 disciples gathered to meet the Lord. "One of the twelve disciples, Thomas (nicknamed the Twin), was not with the others when Jesus came. They told him, 'We have seen the Lord!' But he replied, 'I won't believe it unless I see the nail wounds in his hands, put my fingers into them, and place my hand into the wound in his side'" (John 20:24-25, NLT). Thomas' doubt made him an imperfect disciple, just as many of us are imperfect because of our doubts.

So, what can we learn from imperfect Thomas? "Eight days later the disciples were together again, and this time Thomas was with them" (John 20:26, NLT). Jesus singled out Thomas to tell him to put his finger in the wounds of His hands, and his hand into the wound in His side. But the most important thing Jesus said, "Don't be faithless any longer. Believe!" (John 20:27, NLT). It is then that Thomas made the greatest statement of faith concerning Jesus Christ, "My Lord and my God!" (John 20:28, NLT).

What can you learn from imperfect Thomas? *You may be plagued with doubts that make you an imperfect disciple, but encountering Jesus will transform you. He will forgive you...restore you...and use you.*

NAOMI, A BITTER PUSHY WOMAN, BECOMES A NOURISHER

Naomi was married to Elimelech and they were described as "Ephrathites from Bethlehem" (Ruth 1:2). That phrase suggest they were financially well to do and living among the social elite in their community. When famine came to the Promised Land, they left God's country to settle in a country of idols and false gods. They settled down in Moab to enjoy their exclusive lifestyle. Their two sons, Mahlon and Kilion, married Moabite women. Later, Elimelech died. Then ten years later, both of Naomi's sons died, leaving her with her two daughters-in-law, i.e., Ruth and Orpah.

Naomi had no reason to stay in Moab, having lost everything. She told her two daughters-in-law she was going back to her hometown of Bethlehem. She told them not to call her Naomi, "Instead call me Mara" a word that meant bitter. Her lifestyle goals were gone, and now she was bitter. Naomi told both daughters-in-law to stay in Moab as she returned to the Promised Land. But Ruth said, "Don't ask me to leave you and turn back. Wherever you go, I will go; wherever you live, I will live. Your people will be my people, and your God will be my God" (Ruth 1:16, NLT).

When Naomi and Ruth returned to the Promised Land, God blessed the faith of Ruth and made it possible for her to marry a wealthy property owner, Boaz. When Ruth and Boaz had a son, Obed, he was the grandfather of David, and was in the line of the coming Messiah.

At the end Naomi was more than grandmother, she became the child's caretaker, teaching Obed and training him for spiritual leadership. The women said of the grandson to Naomi, "Praise the Lord, who has now provided a redeemer for your family! ... May he restore your youth" (Ruth 4:14-15, NLT). "Naomi took the baby and cuddled him to her breast. And she cared for him as if he were her own" (Ruth 4:16, NLT).

What can we learn from imperfect Naomi? *The enticement of position and wealth can leave you in poverty, but choosing to follow God's plan for your life will give you fulfillment and usefulness.*

SAMSON—WRONGLY TRUSTED IN HIS OWN STRENGTH

Samson was supernaturally born as a result of God's intervention. The Scriptures says of Samson's mother, "She was unable to become pregnant, and... had no children" (Judges 13:2, NLT). "The angel of the Lord appeared to Manoah" (Judges 13:3, NLT) her husband, and promised a son. Their child was to be raised as Nazirite , meaning "he could not drunk wine, nor strong drink, nor eat anything that is unclean, or cut his hair" (Judges 13:7, ELT).

One more thing about this son. "He will begin to rescue Israel from the Philistines" (Judges 13:5, NLT). Note carefully, he didn't completely deliver Israel from the Philistines only "begin" to get the job done.

Samson's name means *sun*, that identified him with God who was with him, "The Lord blessed him as he grew up. And the Spirit of the Lord began to stir him" (Judges 13:24-25, NLT).

Samson was known for his tremendous physical strength, but it was not just his muscle strength, "The Spirit of the Lord came powerfully upon Samson" (Judges 15:14, NLT). His strength was in God. But Samson's outstanding quality—his physical strength—was not enough to protect him, from sin's temptation by a prostitute named Delilah, and he was destroyed.

What lessons can be learned from imperfect Samson? *You must depend only on God because one strong gift from Him is not enough to protect from temptation and destruction.*

SOLOMON—THE WORLD'S WISEST MADE BAD CHOICES

Solomon became king over all of Israel (Judah and the ten tribes united together). It was then that the Lord appeared to Solomon in a dream at night and said, "What do you want? Ask, and I will give it to you!" (1 Kings 3:5, NLT).

Solomon asked for wisdom, not for money nor for long life. As a result God said, "Behold, I have done according to your words; see, I have given you a wise and understanding heart, so that there has not been anyone like you before you, nor shall any like you arise after you" (1 Kings 3:12). The one thing Solomon asked, was given to him. But his wisdom did not protect him from all of the temptations in life, just as your prominent spiritual gift will not protect you from temptation.

When Solomon became king of all of Israel, he did many things right. He eliminated those who challenged his kingdom and those who compromised the Lord's standards. Solomon built the beautiful temple in Jerusalem, and afterwards it was given his name, *Solomon's Temple*. When Solomon dedicated the temple, "The glory of the Lord had filled the Lord's house. And when all the children of Israel saw...fire came down, and the glory of the Lord on the temple" (2 Chronicles 7:2-3). The greatness of Solomon's wisdom is evidenced by his mighty army, navy, forts and wealth.

God had appeared to Solomon in a dream to give him what he asked, but somewhere along the line, he got off track. He had seven hundred wives, and three hundred concubines. This was his downfall. "But King Solomon loved many strange women, together with the daughter of Pharaoh, women of the Moabites, Ammonites, Edomites, Zidonians, and Hittites" (1 Kings 11:1, KJV). The Lord said, "Ye shall not go in to them, neither shall they come in unto you: for surely they will turn away your heart after their gods" (1 Kings 11:2 KJV). The Scriptures observed, "For it came to pass, when Solomon was old, that his wives turned away his heart after other gods: and his heart was not perfect with the Lord his God" (1 Kings 11:4 KJV). So, what happened? "Then did Solomon build a high place for Chemosh, the abomination of Moab, in the hill that is before Jerusalem, and for Molech, the abomination of the children of Ammon. And likewise did he for all his strange wives, which burnt incense and sacrificed unto their gods" (1 Kings 11:7-8, KJV).

What can we learn from imperfect Solomon? *You can be rich, powerful, smart and even build something outstanding for God—like Solomon's Temple—but if you compromise your marriage and acknowledge foreign gods and worship them, you can destroy everything you have accomplished.*

RICH YOUNG RULER—A WEALTHY MAN LEARNED VALUE

The Rich Young Ruler came asking Jesus the right question, "What shall I do to inherit eternal life?" (Luke 18:18). He told Jesus he had kept all of the commandments from his youth up. But Jesus knew his heart and said, "There is still one thing you haven't done. Sell all your possessions and give the money to the poor, and you will have treasure in heaven. Then come, follow me" (Luke 18:22, NLT). "But when the man heard this he became very sad, for he was very rich" (Luke 18:23, NLT).

"Looking at the man, Jesus felt genuine love for him" (Luke 10:21, NLT). Jesus loves everyone, but He especially loves those who come to Him sincerely as did the Rich Young Ruler. What did the love of Jesus accomplish? History teaches us that the apostle Barnabas who sold all that he had and gave to the poor, was actually the Rich Young Ruler. The Bible teaches, "Barnabas...sold a field he owned and brought the money to the apostles" (Acts 4:37, NLT).

From the Rich Young Ruler/Barnabas we learned you may be so wrapped up in your money that you might reject Jesus' first claim on your life, but when you respond positively to His love, you sacrifice all to follow Him. Then Jesus can use you in ways you never imagined.

SAUL/PAUL—THE CONSUMMATE LEGALIST FINALLY GAINS PERFECTION

Of all the notable people who tried to live a perfect life—and came close to doing it—it was Saul the unsaved rabbi. He persecuted the church and attacked any Jew who didn't live by his standards because they turned from "law keeping" to the saving grace of Jesus Christ. Saul's perfection (Philippians 3:4-6) was self-recognized. When Saul was converted, eventually his name was changed to Paul (literally, small one), then he recognized his sinfulness, i.e., imperfection (Romans 7:11-19). Only in Jesus Christ was Paul justified, which means he was declared perfect not made perfect. *From Saul/Paul we learn that any imperfect people—you—can be declared righteous or perfect in God's sight. Then the good works you do in the flesh, can now become your ministry through the power of Christ Jesus.*

WRAP UP

If you have tried to serve God but failed, I have good news for you. Through imperfection you can call on God to use you and equip you for service. You can ask for cleansing by the blood of Christ who will forgive all your imperfections (sins) (1 John 1:7). You can yield to Jesus Christ for His power to work through you. You can ask the Holy Spirit to guide you and give you authority in ministry.

PART ONE

LEARNING FROM GOD'S IMPERFECT PEOPLE

Chapter 1

JACOB

A Liar And Trickster Changed By A Dream

IF God ever used an imperfect person, it was Jacob, grandson of Abraham the father of the Jews. Even the name Jacob meant "surplanter" or "trickster." But his name was changed to Israel and today God's nation—the Jewish people—are called by Jacob's new name, Israelites. And God's nation is known by his new name—Israel.

Even before Jacob was born, he was attempting to "surplant" his older brother Esau. The Lord told Jacob's mother Rebekah, "The sons in your womb will become two nations. From the very beginning, the two nations will be rivals. One nation will be stronger than the other; and your older son will serve your younger son" (Genesis 25:23, NLT). The first son born was Esau, meaning *red* in Hebrew.. He was covered with red hair at birth. "Then the other twin was born with his hand grasping Esau's heel. So they named him Jacob" (Genesis 25:26, NLT).

When we first see the brothers together, they are "contending" for superiority. Esau had been hunting, but was not successful. When he returned home Jacob had been cooking stew. The Bible describes Esau as "exhausted and hungry" (Genesis 25:29, NLT). Esau asked for some of the red stew that Jacob was cooking. Jacob replied, "All right...but trade me your rights as the firstborn son" (Genesis 25:31, NLT).

Jacob would not give him the stew until he made Esau swear the birthright to him, thereby declaring that Jacob had all legal rights as the firstborn in the family.

Next, Jacob deceived his father to get a financial inheritance of the family. "Isaac was old and turning blind" (Genesis 27:1, NLT). So, he told his older son, Esau, to go kill some game and come prepare (cook or bar-b-que) his favorite dish for him. "Then I will pronounce the blessing that belongs to you, my firstborn son, before I die" (Genesis 27:4, NLT).

The root of Jacob's deceptions was learned from his mother. The Bible says, "But Rebekah overheard what Isaac had said to his son Esau…she said to her son Jacob" (Genesis 27:5-6, NLT). Rebekah devised a scheme to deceive Isaac and get the inheritance for Jacob.

The story is well known.

Instead of using spicy wild game, mother and son killed young goats, cooked the meat the way Isaac liked it, and got it ready to take to him. Then Rebekah took goat skin to cover Jacob's arms. Even when Jacob complained, "Esau is a hairy man, and my skin is smooth" (Genesis 27:11, NLT). Rebekah's response, "Just do what I tell you" (Genesis 27:13, NLT).

Jacob walked into his father's tent with the stewed goat's meat and deceived him. He pretended he was Esau, even wearing gloves and sleeves with goat hair. Even when his father said, "The voice is Jacob's, but the hands are Esau's" (Genesis 27:22, NLT).

Jacob received the pledge of inheritance from his father and left. When Esau came in and found out he had been deceived, he said, "No wonder his name is Jacob, for now he has cheated me twice. First he took my rights as the firstborn, and now he has stolen my blessing (inheritance)" (Genesis 27:36, NLT).

But the story does not end there, Esau let it be known his hatred for his brother. "Esau began to scheme, 'I will soon be mourning my father's death. Then I will kill my brother, Jacob'" (Genesis 27:41, NLT). Jacob had to leave home to keep from being killed by his brother Esau.

A DREAM CHANGED JACOB'S FOCUS : GENESIS 28-32, NLT

Jacob left home, heading for the Tigris Euphrates Valley to find Laban, his family relative. That first night he set up camp and used a stone as a pillow and laid down to sleep. It was then that he dreamed and saw a stairway (some call it a ladder) that reached from earth up to heaven. On the ladder he saw angels going up and down the stairway.

"At the top of the stairway stood the Lord, and he said, 'I am the Lord, the God of your grandfather Abraham, and the God of your father, Isaac. The ground you are lying on belongs to you. I am giving it to you and your descendants. Your descendants will be as numerous as the dust of the earth! They will spread out in all directions—to the west and the east, to the north and the south. And all the families of the earth will be blessed through you and your descendants. What's more, I am with you, and I will protect you wherever you go. One day I will bring you back to this land. I will not leave you until I have finished giving you everything I have promised you'" (Genesis 28:13-15).

It is interesting to study that later God changed his name from Jacob (the deceiver) to Israel (prince with God). The land promised to him is not called after his name Jacob, but after his new name, i.e., the land of Israel.

Jacob spent twenty years in the Tigris Euphrates Valley. He married two women, first Leah, then Rachel. He had ten sons from Leah and two from Rachel, and she died giving birth to the second son, Benjamin.

Just as Jacob deceived his father, so according to his nature, Jacob deceived his father-in-law Laban (Genesis 30:25-43).

Because Jacob deceived his father-in-law to get wealthy, Laban's sons also were mad at Jacob, thinking that he was getting wealthy with money that they should be getting. "He has gained all his wealth at our father's expense" (Genesis 31:1).

Jacob took his two wives, twelve sons and one daughter, plus all of his wealth and herds, and left security to return back home to the Promised Land When Laban and his sons found out, they chased after Jacob, catching him at Mizpah. That was half-way home. There was a great argument between the two.

Jacob argued, "I worked for you through the scoring heat of the day and through cold and sleepless nights. Yes, for twenty years I slaved in your house! I worked for fourteen years earning your two daughters, and then six more years for your flock. And you changed my wages ten times! In fact, if the God of my father had not been on my side—the God of Abraham and the fearsome God of Isaac—you would have sent me away empty-handed. But God had seen your abuse and my hard work. That is why He appeared to you last night and rebuked you."

Jacob and Laban made an agreement called the Mizpah Benediction. It has been used harmoniously for years as a benediction in Christian youth rallies. But when originally agreed upon, it was a peace treaty between two people who did not trust each other, "The Lord watch between me and thee, when we are absent one from another." (Genesis 31:49, KJV).

Jacob continued toward his home and then heard that his brother Esau was coming toward him with 400 armed men. "Esau...is already on his way to meet you—with an army of 400 men" (Genesis 32:6).

The imperfect Jacob tried to deceive his brother again. He divided his flocks into two groups, sending one ahead, and keeping part back with him thinking if angry Esau takes revenge he can take or steal the first set of flocks and servants. Perhaps "crafty Jacob" is thinking if he steals both the first and second sets of flocks and servants, he can still escape with his life.

When Jacob crosses the river Jabbok (northern boundary to the Promised Land), he is alone in a tent at night waiting for the dawn when he would meet his angry brother. Did Jacob pray? What did he expect? Then he heard a noise outside the tent. Was it a man, an intruder? Jacob did not know who he was. Did Jacob think the man was his brother? Did he think the man was sent by Laban to kill him? The man was unknown to Jacob. He wrestled with that man all night.

Remember wrestling was a "passing activity" of shepherds as they were watching their sheep. They wrestled one another to find out who was the best, who could pin the other. And so Jacob and the man started wrestling, just as shepherds might do.

Did Jacob think the man was his brother Esau who had come to kill him, or someone sent by his brother?

Jacob did not know who the man was, or what his intent was; all he knew he must fight for his life.

That night in the tent Jacob wrestled with God. Actually, the intruder in the tent is not identified as God until after the morning sun had come up and Jacob said, "I have seen God face to face" (Genesis 32:30).

Obviously the wrestling match was more than just wanting to claim victory. To Jacob, it was a battle of life and death.

Because they wrestled all night, the intruder could not prevail. "When the man saw that he would not win the match, he touched Jacob's hip and wrenched it out of its socket. Then the man said, 'Let me go, for the dawn is breaking!'" (Genesis 32:25-26).

Here Jacob's faith came to the foreground. Does he remember the dream he had with God twenty years earlier? Did he realize this was God who could bless his life?

Jacob give a condition, "I will not let you go unless you bless me" (Genesis 32:26).

It is here that Jacob's name is changed, and more than changing his name, perhaps the entire focus in life was permanently changed.

"'What is your name?' the man asked. He replied, 'Jacob.' 'Your name will no longer be Jacob,' the man told him. 'From now on you will be called Israel, because you have fought with God and with men and have won'" (Genesis 32:27-28). Today, many people may wrestle with God, but not physically - it is in their minds and through their emotions, often over an issue or decision. But Jacob did actually wrestle God Himself.

"Jacob named the place Peniel (which means 'face of God'), for he said, 'I have seen God face to face, yet my life has been spared'" (Genesis 32:30).

LESSONS TO TAKE AWAY

Are you an imperfect believer like Jacob? If so, what do you need from God? First you need a dream. You need to be reminded of who you are, and you must keep your focus on God's future for your life. That dream will keep you going through hard times, difficulties and also through the good times. But also a dream will motivate you and empower you to continue planning and working toward the goal God has set for your life.

Second, your encounter with God must demonstrate to God your determination to serve Him, to please Him and make Him number one in your life. Also, your encounter with God must let God touch you, so that you can see His face, and as a result you can go out to minister and serve Him as He wants you to serve Him.

Chapter 2

NOAH

After Walking With God, He Got Drunk

NOAH is listed in Hebrews 11 – the New Testament Hall of Faith – as one of those who lived and ministered by faith (Hebrews 11:7). He is further identified as one of only two antediluvians who were described as "walked with God" (Genesis 6:9; cf. 5:24). In contrast to the wickedness of his age, God trusted Noah to save humanity and salvage the world after the flood, or at least that part of the world worth salvaging.

"Noah was a just man, perfect in his generations" (6:9). He understood the need for both faith and works. He is described as a *just man*, i.e., one who was justified by God, suggesting expressed faith in God, for by faith a man is justified (Romans 5:1). On the practical side, Noah's life was exemplary he is described as "perfect in his generations." His deep faith in God was evidenced by his works. He both built the ark and warned others of the coming judgement. The apostle Peter described Noah as "a preacher of righteousness" (2 Peter 2:5). Certainly his lifestyle gave authority to his message.

But even the great faith of Noah was not able to keep him from sinning against God—drunkenness—and as a result, Noah hurt his grandson—Canaan. In this one act illustrated in Scriptures (Genesis 9:20-27), Canaan and his family were infected with a sin—a sin so great—that eventually God had the Canaanites driven from the land and exterminated. Thus, Noah was another imperfect person, and we can learn a lesson from his imperfection.

There is some difference of opinion as to the duration of Noah's pre-Flood ministry. Some commentators believe it lasted 120 years assuming Noah began his ministry of building the ark and warning the people of a coming end to the race (Genesis 6:3). On the other hand, Noah's sons were only a hundred years old when they entered the ark, and then appear to have been married before God assigned Noah the task of saving humanity (v. 18). Regardless of the duration of his ministry, all are agreed as to its results. Apart from his wife, sons, and their wives, Noah was apparently unsuccessful in convincing any others of joining his family on the ark.

The greatest evidence of faith in the life of Noah was the building of an ark. Two significant facts help to better understand the extent of Noah's faith. First, it had never before rained on the earth. Noah himself was apparently not told of the rain until the final week of loading the ark (7:4). He simply believed God would flood the world without understanding the means God would use to produce the water.

The second unusual fact about the ark is its size. Scholars debate the size of a cubit described as either eighteen or twenty-two inches long. By these standards the ark was 450/550 feet long, 75/91.6 feet wide and 45/55 feet high. In the history of navigation, only within the last 250 years have men begun building ships that large. Some writers suggest that Noah's ability to build such a large seaworthy vessel is an indication as to how advanced the pre-Flood civilization must have been.

THE JUDGMENT WATERS: GENESIS 7-9

After the ark was completed, God invited Noah and his family to come aboard. Apparently it took a full week to get everyone and everything aboard. Assuming the food supplies were already aboard, there were still two of every unclean animal and seven of every clean animal that came aboard the ark (Genesis 7:2; 8:9). According to the estimates of Morris and Whitcomb (*The Genesis Flood*, Baker, 1961) this involved about 35,000 individual animals representing all of the known species of animals today. Because many of these were small, they suggest there was no difficulty holding all of them in the ark. The care of these animals on the ark may have been greatly simplified if the animals engaged in hibernation, as do many species of animals today.

When the ark was completely loaded, "the Lord shut him in" (Genesis 7:16). That same day it began to rain. The resulting rain caused not only the flood, but also the flood was caused by the release of subterranean bodies of water, described as "the fountains of the deep" (v. 11). The eruption of these fountains seems to imply an explosion. The tremendous pressure of water on the face of the earth would cause mudslides and changes in its terrain including changing the existence of mountains. All human life except Noah and his family was destroyed. All animal life disappeared. The horrendous results was evidence of the judgment by God.

Even before the flood, Noah and his sons and their wives appear to have chosen to live together as an extended family. After the Flood, Noah became a grandfather as his three sons had sons of their own. Probably at this point, Noah and his sons became ranchers, slowly traveling south with their herds and flocks as they grazed in the open pastures. Eventually, Noah began to feel old with all his grandchildren running around or maybe he was just tired of the constant traveling involved in a nomadic lifestyle. For whatever reason, the time came when Noah settled for a somewhat tranquil lifestyle, and again changed his occupation from being a carpenter. "And Noah began to be a farmer, and he planted a vineyard" (Genesis 9:20).

The Scriptures record Noah's farming career in one tragic harvest season. It began when "he drank of the wine and was drunk" (v. 21). Over the years both Jewish and Christian commentators have tried to be kind to Noah, noting this is the first mention of wine in the Scriptures and suggesting Noah may not have known the beverage would have an alcoholic content that produced drunkenness. But in light of the New Testament revelation of drinking in the days of Noah before the Flood (Matthew 24:38), this excuse hardly holds water. Noah was the patriarch of his family and as such should have known what Solomon later learned: "It is not for kings, O Lemuel, it is not for kings to drink wine, nor for princes intoxicating drink" (Proverbs 31:4). Did Noah change in his spiritual commitment over the years? Had he drifted from God? Was his gradual wandering from

God imperceptible to the casual observer? But now, years after Noah's great victory over the flood, it was evident that the Noah who raised the wineskin to his lips and got drunk, was not the same Noah who, "was a just man, perfect in his generations" (6:9).

As Noah lay naked in a drunken stupor, "Ham, the father of Canaan, saw the nakedness of his father, and told his two brothers outside" (9:22). Because Noah later cursed Canaan, it was probably Canaan who first "saw" Noah and told his father Ham what happened. When Shem and Japheth learned of Noah's state, they grabbed a garment; perhaps Noah's own garment that Ham had presented as evidence of his claims, that he was both drunk and naked. Shem and Japheth apparently walked into the tent backward, with his coat held to their eyes, "and covered the nakedness of their father" (v. 23).

When Noah finally recovered from the effects of his wine, he realized what had happened. Noah cursed Canaan and blessed Shem and Japheth and their descendants. Under the conditions of Noah's statement, the descendants of Canaan, the Canaanites, were designated to be servants of the descendants of Shem. Canaan lived in the land of Canaan which became the Israel of our day. They did not become part of the black peoples of Africa and the curse has nothing to do with the servitude of black races. Canaan became servant to Shem when Joshua conquered the Promised Land and defeated the Canaanites.

LESSONS TO TAKE AWAY

One can be greatly used by God, but because all humans have a sinful nature, that person can violate their communion with God. Apparently, Noah not only did what was wrong, he was guilty of the same evil he preached against. Therefore, remember the Scriptures, "If you think you are standing strong, be careful not to fall" (1 Corinthians 10;12, NLT). If

righteous Noah could fall, it could happen to anyone. The Bible warns "be careful," not to fall into the evil you once opposed.

A second lesson is also present here: many years of godly living and being used of God in a powerful way will not automatically make you immune to temptation. Your successful experience is not a guarantee of future successful living or future usefulness in serving God. The only guarantee is your daily walk with God, or to put it even more practically, your only guarantee is your moment by moment walk with God.

Some people fall at their weak points; they surrender to evil because they are tempted in an area where they are most vulnerable. But Noah should have been strong against drunkenness because he preached against it prior to the flood. *The Bible by Jesus* says, "People went on eating, drinking, getting married until the flood came" (Matthew 24:38, Bible by Jesus). One of the sins that caused the flood, was a sin that tripped up Noah at the end of his life.

Your sin can have devastating results on your family. Noah got drunk and his two sons—Shem and Japhet—tried to cover up their father's problem. They did it with a garment. The other son Ham apparently didn't know what to do. The son of Ham, Canaan, was the one who apparently discovered his grandfather drunk and naked. When Noah awoke, he put a curse on Canaan. It was a judgment that played out over the years when those living in Canaan were judged by God and driven out of the Holy Land or were destroyed in a number of wars or fighting. The lesson—your sin does more than harm your testimony, it can harm the "weaker brother," and/or members of your family (1 Corinthians 8:9-13).

Chapter 3

PETER

A Granite Rock Chipped

ONE of the strongest voices for Jesus Christ in the early church was Simon Peter. It would be difficult to preach to the people of Jerusalem when most of the city had supported the decisions of the leaders to crucify Jesus on the cross. But Peter was the boldest among the disciples. He stood before a vast crowd at Pentecost to challenge them, "You nailed Him to a cross and killed Him" (Acts 2:23, NLT). He challenged them, "Each one of you must repent of your sins and turn to God and be baptized in the name of Jesus Christ" (Acts 2:38, NLT). Over 3,000 were saved on that occasion.

Peter was filled with the Holy Spirit (2:4) and Jesus used him mightily to establish His church. But remember this is the same Peter who denied Jesus and ran away with the other disciples when the solders arrested Jesus in the Garden of Gethsemane. Even though bold and powerfully used, Peter was an imperfect vessel.

Even when Peter was first invited by his brother Andrew to come meet Jesus Christ, Peter resisted. His imperfect disposition was revealed even then, The Bible says Andrew found Peter and "brought" him to Jesus. The Greek verb *heuriskei,* translated "brought" (John 1:42), implies resistance. Andrew had to search for and persuade Peter to come meet Jesus.

While the Scriptures do not tell the actual words Simon used to resist coming to Jesus, it suggests he was not eager to respond. The word "brought" implies constraint was used by Andrew because Peter was unwilling. Perhaps a better expression is, "He dragged him to Jesus." But it was this meeting that would forever change his life.

One of the first things Jesus did when he met Simon was change his name. Jesus realized how out of character his name was—*Simon* in Hebrew is *Simeon,* meaning listener. Peter was not a listener but a talker, an impulsive leader.

The Greek word *emblepsas,* translated "looked" (John 1:42), describes Jesus' penetrating stare that looked "right through" to see Peter as he really was. It was the same look Jesus would give Peter more than three years later on the night when Peter swore he never knew Jesus. On that occasion Peter was overcome with guilt which led to a night of bitter weeping (Luke 22:61-62).

In that first meeting between Jesus and Peter, the Lord saw what others missed; Jesus renamed Simon Cephas or Peter, meaning "a stone."

A number of things were involved in that name change. First in giving Peter a new name, Jesus was subtly telling Simon it was not enough that he came to meet Him. Jesus was declaring that He had control of Peter's life, and therefore the right to rename him. Second, Jesus was telling Peter that He would transform him. The name Cephas is Aramaic, meaning "rock." That is also the meaning of the Greek name Peter. If Peter resembled a rock at all, it was little more than sandstone. Later, Peter was told he could become a building stone in the temple Jesus would build (1 Peter 2:5). By calling him Cephas, Jesus was challenging Peter to live up to the strength of that name.

JESUS: OFFERED HONOR TO A HUMBLED FOLLOWER: LUKE 5:1-11

Jesus had met Peter at that first occasion, but Peter had not yet become a follower—disciple—of Jesus. Later, a crowd was following Jesus when He was walking on the shore of the Sea of Galilee. Jesus saw four fishermen, Peter, Andrew, James, and John, who had been fishing all night without success. When Jesus spotted the boat and recognized the owners, it was just what He needed to help keep the masses at a distance so He could teach them. So Jesus sat in Peter's boat.

After teaching the multitudes, Jesus encouraged Peter to launch out into deeper water and let down his net for a catch (Luke 5:4). Peter agreed to throw in one net (Luke 5:5) probably expecting little if any fish. No sooner had the net been thrown into the water than it was filled with a large school of fish. It was so full that the net actually began to break. James

and John were called to help. The boat was so full of fish it began to take on water, and still there seemed to be no end to the fish.

Then Peter recognized Jesus was more than a rabbi. He was the One the Old Testament prophet called *Lord* of *Jehovah*, the personal God who delighted in forgiving sin. And as he realized who Jesus was, he was also deeply conscious of who he was. He fell on his knees before Jesus, "Depart from me, for I am a sinful man, O Lord!" (Luke 5:8).

The term Lord means one who would possess; Jesus would be Peter's owner. Peter would be the slave but there was nothing to fear from Jesus. He turned to encourage Peter, "Do not be afraid. From now on you will catch men" (Luke 5:10). Peter and the others would be disciples of Jesus. "So, when they had brough their boats to land, they forsook all and followed Him" (Luke 5:11). From this moment on, Peter would no longer split his energies between fishing and following Jesus. Peter would be a dedicated disciple.

JESUS POINTS OUT PETER'S PROBLEM: MATTHEW 16:13-23

When Jesus and His disciples arrived north of the Sea of Galilee at Caesarea-Philippi, He asked His disciples two questions. The first was, "who do men say that I, the son of Man am?" (Matthew 16:13). When Jesus asked this question, He used His human designation, "Son of Man." They answered He was viewed in the same company as the prophets like Elijah or Jeremiah. Then He asked a second question, "But who do you say that I am?" Peter responded, "You are the Christ, the son of the living God" (Matthew 16:16). Peter used the title of deity to describe Jesus, "Son of God."

This has been called his greatest statement of faith. Jesus explained that Peter's conclusion about His deity was a revelation given him by His Father. Then He added, "And I also say to you that you are Peter, and on this rock I will build My church, and the gates of Hades shall not prevail against it" (Matthew 16:18).

This statement introduces the church. It didn't appear in the Old Testament, and Jesus had not used this term. Some claim Jesus meant the church would be established by Peter whose name meant "a stone." But Peter himself identified Jesus as the rock upon which the church would be built (cf. 1 Peter 2:7).

In this first mention of the church in Scripture, Jesus explained the church would prevail against the gates of Hades. Gates were perceived to be the strength of a city, yet even the strength of hell and the unseen world could not stop the ever-advancing Christian church. As this church faithfully proclaimed the gospel, it will use the keys of the kingdom of heaven to set people free from the bondage of sin (Matthew 16:19). Failure to share the Good News (the gospel) was to bind people in their sins both now and for eternity.

As Jesus introduced this concept of the church to His disciples, His ministry distinctly changed. "From that time Jesus began to show to His disciples that He must go to Jerusalem, and suffer many things from the elders and chief priests and scribes, and be killed, and be raised the third day" (Matthew 16:21). He had earlier mentioned the cross in His ministry, but not as explicitly as now.

The idea of their leader being crucified was revolting to the disciples. The fact that crucifixion was a common form of execution at that time did not minimize the horror associated with the practice. Peter objected to the idea of Jesus being crucified. "Far be it from You, Lord; this shall not happen to you!" he argued with Jesus (Matthew 16:22).

"Get behind Me, Satan!" (Matthew 16:23). Jesus called Peter the name of His ultimate enemy. While Peter's intention may have been noble - to save Jesus from a horrible way to die - it would also accomplish the will of Satan by preventing Jesus from fulfilling the greatest aspect of His messianic work, i.e., He died for the sins of the world.

PETER—THE IMPERFECT DISCIPLE—DENIED THE LORD: LUKE 22:54-62

On the night when Jesus was being tried, Peter denied his Lord. When Peter came to the place where the trial took place, a servant girl responsible for the door asked, "You are not also one of this Man's disciples, are you?" (John 18:17). Her question suggests she thought Peter was a follower of Jesus. She probably intended the question to mock or ridicule Peter rather than expose him. But the disciple responded quickly, "I am not" (John 18:17). Peter's denials of Jesus had begun. On two more occasions, Peter denied the Lord. The last time, Peter cursed.

Earlier that evening Jesus warned Peter he would deny Him at least three times (Luke 22:61; Mark 14:30). As Jesus was being taken from the high priest's home to go to Pilate's residence, Jesus turned to look at Peter (Mark 14:72; Luke 22:61). The sound of the cock crowing and the look of Jesus caused Peter to remember the warning Jesus had spoken earlier that evening. Peter had denied the Lord, now he knew that Jesus knew. Peter retreated to spend the rest of the evening alone weeping over what he had done. This identifies Peter as an imperfect disciple.

THE RESTITUTION OF PETER: JOHN 21:1-19

Around three weeks after the resurrection, the disciples left Jerusalem, where Jesus had met them in the Upper Room twice. They went to Galilee where Jesus had instructed He would meet them. Peter decided to go fishing and six disciples went with him. They met Jesus who gave them a net full of fishes. Afterward on the shore they had breakfast.

After the meal, Jesus and Peter engaged in a brief conversation. Jesus asked Peter, "Simon, son of Jonah, do you love (*agape*) Me more than these?" (John 21:15). Peter responded, "Yes, Lord; You know that I love (*phileo*) You" (John 21:15). Peter used the friendship word for love. Then Jesus directed Peter, "Keep on feeding my little lambs" (John 21:15, author's translation).

Jesus' first question was followed by a second similar question. Jesus again asked, "Simon, son of Jonah, do you love (*agape*) Me?" using the deeper meaning of love. Peter again responded, "Yes, Lord; You know that I love (*phileo*) You" (John 21:16). Again using only the friendship term. This second time, Jesus told Peter, "Keep on shepherding the young sheep" (John 21:16, author's translation).

A third time, Jesus asked Peter using the friendship term originally used by Peter, "Simon, son of Jonah, do you love (*phileo*) Me?" (John 21:17). Peter was grieved that Jesus continued to question him concerning his love for his Lord and responded, "Lord, You know (*oida*—to know intuitively) all things; You know (*ginosko*—to know experientially) that I only love (*phileo*) You" (John 21:17). This may have been the most honest response in Peter's life. This time Jesus responded to Peter's answer with the directive, "Keep on feeding the mature sheep" (John 21:17, author's translation).

That day on the beach, Peter also learned how his own life would end. A few weeks earlier he had told Jesus he was willing to go to the cross with Him (John 13:37), but then later denied even knowing Jesus. But the day would come when Peter would go to a cross for Him. Jesus predicted, "Most assuredly, I say to you, when you were younger, you girded yourself and walked where you wished; but when you are old, you will stretch out your hands, and another will gird you and carry you where you do not wish," Jesus explained (John 21:18). Then, knowing Peter knew exactly what he would encounter in a life of discipleship, Jesus repeated two words He had first spoken to this disciple almost four years earlier, "Follow me" (John 21:19).

Peter was called a rock (Matthew 16:19), but the rock was a reference to his statement and belief that Christ was the rock in whom he believed. On many occasions Peter stood like a rock for Jesus Christ, but on other occasions, the rock was chipped. Those chips reveal the imperfection of Peter.

When we look at Peter's human personality, we see his "hard headed" reaction to life. Peter was not a "lukewarm" disciple, either he was hot, or he was not. What was Peter—an imperfect disciple. He chipped on occasions.

LESSONS TO TAKE AWAY

Simon was the leader among the 12 disciples while Jesus was alive, but he spoke on the Day of Pentecost, which is considered the *beginning* or *introduction* of the church to Israel and/or the whole world. Approximately 3,000 were saved, baptized and added to the church. Obviously, Peter was God's leader that ushered in God's new institution—the church—to the world. While applauding Peter, remember he was an imperfect man. He was the one rebuked by Jesus because Peter didn't want Jesus to die. Peter uses the one who denied Jesus—as Jesus was on trial—and ended his denial with a curse. Yet, Christ forgave him and used him. Isn't that encouraging to you in your imperfection?

But even after being forgiven, Peter the Rock continued to chip away at his reputation. God gave him a vision of a sheet being lowered from heaven with unclean animals—a symbol of going to the Gentiles—Peter told the Lord, "Not so, Lord" (Acts 9:14). Can a follower of Jesus be an obedient believer when he uses "not" and "Lord" in the same sentence? Is this a sign of imperfect Peter? If it is, then God used Peter to carry the gospel to Cornelius' household where many were saved and the Holy Spirit was poured out on them (Acts 10:44-48). Does that mean God may have a great work for you after you tell him "no"?

Chapter 4

GIDEON

God Pushed An Introvert To Victory

PERHAPS of all the leaders in this book, Gideon thought he was the most imperfect of all to be used by God. When God challenged Gideon, he said, "How can I rescue Israel? My clan is the weakest in the whole tribe of Manasseh, and I am the least in my entire family!" (Judges 6:15, NLT).

However, remember God uses imperfect people. Let's deal with the question. Who determines if they are imperfect? Some outsiders may say one person is imperfect, but they really don't know the inner strength of that person. Others may think a person is imperfect because they know him, and he doesn't measure up in any of the areas. Also some may think they personally are imperfect because of environmental factors, i.e., their birth, family, conditions of their childhood, lack of wealth, or their social standing in society.

Perhaps of all the imperfect people in this book, Gideon had the least ego strength, the weakest self-perception. He was an introvert. He just didn't think he was fit for the job and he demonstrated it in four different ways before God used him to deliver Israel from the Midianites.

THE CRISIS AND GOD'S CALL: JUDGES 6:1-24, NLT

God's people in the land of promise were being overrun by raiding tribes or hordes of desert vandals—Midianites—who swept in to kill...rob...destroy...and then carry their "loot" back to the desert. These herdsmen attacking on fast galloping camels swept through villages and farmlands destroying everything in sight, leaving crops devastated, home destroyed and everything in ruins.

The Bible describes, "Marauders...would attack Israel, camping in the land and destroying crops as far as Gaza. They left the Israelites with nothing to eat, taking all the sheep, goats, camels, cattle and donkeys, these enemy hordes with their livestock were as thick as locus; they arrived on droves of camels too numerous to count and they stayed until the land was stripped bare. Then the Israelites cried out to the Lord for help" (Judges 6:3-6).

The Lord descended into this desperate scene to confront Gideon. "Then the angel of the Lord came and sat beneath the great tree at Ophrah, which belonged to Joash of the clan of Abiezrite. Gideon son of Joash was threshing wheat at the bottom of a winepress to hide the grain from the Midianites" (Judges 6:11).

This is a pitiful scene. Usually wheat threshing was done high on a hillside where the wind would blow away the chaff from the grains of wheat or barley. A person would take a stick to beat the wheat while still in the husk, the purpose of which was to separate the grains of wheat from the shell. Then both would be tossed into the air, using either a shovel or a flat board to let the wind blow away the husk and leaves. The heaver grains fell to the ground. But Gideon knew if he was threshing wheat on the hillside, he would be spotted by the Midianites who would come steal everything and perhaps take his life.

So, Gideon was hiding in a winepress. This is a low spot dug out of the ground and lined with stones where grapes are pressed into wine. Usually this low area was cool to preserve the richness of the grapes. In the bottom of a winepress they would stomp on the grapes, separating the juice from the hull. The area was usually protected from sunlight so the wine would not ferment ahead of time and spoil. A perfect place for a coward to hide.

The angel of the Lord appeared to Gideon. Many have called him a Christophany, which is an appearance of God, i.e., Christ. Listen to the irony of the greetings as the angel of the Lord speak to Gideon.

"Mighty hero, the Lord is with you" (Judges 6:12).

Today we would call this a slam or put-down. Why? Gideon is not a hero, he is hiding. He is not

a man of valor, he is a coward, and he is hiding from the Midianites out of sight. So, when the angel of the Lord called him a valiant man of God, Gideon is really an imperfect man, not qualified to be a leader.

It is here that the skeptical Gideon asks a question. "If the Lord is with us, why has all this happened to us? And where are all the miracles our ancestors told us about? Didn't they say, 'The Lord brought us up out of Egypt'? But now the Lord has abandoned us and handed us over to the Midianites" (Judges 6:13).

In this encounter the angel of the Lord challenges Gideon, "Go with the strength you have, and rescue Israel from the Midianites. I am sending you!" (Judges 6:14).

In response, Gideon claims to have no strength, and makes excuses for himself, "how can I rescue Israel? My clan is the weakest in the whole tribe of Manasseh, and I am the least in my entire family!" (Judges 6:15).

It is here that the Lord challenges Gideon and gives him a reason why he will win a great victory. "I will be with you. And you will destroy the Midianites as if you were fighting against one man" (Judges 6:16).

Remember, Gideon was weak and had little or no self-confidence, and he asked the angel of the Lord to prove what was just said, "If you are truly going to help me, show me a sign to prove that it is really the Lord speaking to me" (Judges 6:17).

At this point Gideon tells the angel to remain as he runs to his home to get a sacrifice to present to the Lord God. Gideon recognizes that when approaching God—as all Israelites in the Old Testament—he must bring a sacrifice.

"He cooked a young goat, and with a basket of flour he baked some bread without yeast. Then, carrying the meat in a basket and the broth in a pot, he brought them out and presented them to the angel, who was under the great tree" (Judges 6:19).

Remember Gideon is not from the Levitical family, and he is not the head of a great family. Let's ask a question. Does he understand the role of making a sacrifice for God? It is here that the angel of the Lord says to him, "Place the meat and the unleavened bread on this rock, and pour the broth over it" (Judges 6:20). This is a picture of making an offering to God.

Then, to verify his challenge to Gideon, the angel of the Lord produced a miracle. "Then the angel of the Lord touched the meat and bread with the tip of the staff in his hand, and fire flamed up from the rock and consumed all he had brought. And the angel of the Lord disappeared" (Judges 6:21).

At this point Gideon realizes that he is dealing with the sovereign Lord who has appeared to him and challenged him to go and fight the Midianites. He cries out, "I have seen the angel of the Lord face to face!" (Judges 6:22, NLT).

As a result Gideon built an altar to the Lord at the spot and named it Yahweh-Shalom (which means *the Lord is peace*) (Judges 6:24). And when the book of Judges was written that altar was still used as place of sacrificing to the Lord God.

FIRST CONFIRMATION: JUDGES 6:25-35, NLT

That night the Lord said to Gideon, "Take the second bull from your father's herd, the one that is seven years old. Pull down your father's altar to Baal, and cut down the Asherah pole standing beside it. Then build an altar to the Lord your God here on this hilltop sanctuary, laying the stones carefully. Sacrifice the bull as a burnt offering on the altar, using as fuel the wood of the Asherah pole you cut down" (Judges 6:25-26).

Because Gideon was fearful, he did it at night, taking servants from his father's house to help him complete the job overnight.

The next morning, the people in town discovered the altar of Baal had been broken down and the Asherah pole had been cut down and used for firewood; then they saw a new altar had built and used as a sacrifice to the Lord. They began searching for the person who did this. After a careful search they found it was Gideon who had done all these things. They demanded of his father,

"Bring out your son...he must die" (Judges 6:30).

Gideon had made a life-threating leap of faith in destroying the altar to a fake god in obedience to the living God. Now his life was threatened.

But the logical father said. "If Baal truly is a god, let him defend himself" (Judges 6:31).

As a result of this confrontation with heathen idols and the townsfolk, Gideon got a nickname. He became known as *Baal fighter*.

SECOND CONFIRMATION: JUDGES 6:36-40, NLT

In the first confrontation, it was God who initiated the contact when He told Gideon what to do. This time, Gideon initiates the confrontation. He prays to God, "If you are truly going to use me to rescue Israel as you promised, prove it to me in this way. I will put a wool fleece on the threshing floor tonight. If the fleece is wet with dew in the morning but the ground is dry, then I will know that you are going to help me rescue Israel as you promised" (Judges 6:36-37).

Technically, Gideon was praying for a miracle. He was going to put a dry wool fleece out on the threshing floor at nighttime. Then in the morning if it was wet from dew, it would prove to him God had done something. But that was not really a challenge, because porous wool naturally absorbs moisture from wet air, i.e., dew. So, the next morning the wool was wet. That is not a miracle—the same would happen if we tried it today in the same conditions. Gideon had second-guessed himself.

So, he prayed, "Please don't be angry with me, but let me make one more request. Let me use the fleece for one more test. This time let the fleece remain dry while the ground around it is wet with dew" (Judge 6:39). This would demonstrate the miraculous, because porous wool would attract moisture if the ground around it was wet. But if the wool was dry and the ground was wet, it would show God had intervened in a natural process. So, "the fleece was dry in the morning, but the ground was covered with dew" (Judges 6:40).

Some Christians have asked for God's guidance or leadership by putting out a fleece. That means they pray about a matter, asking God to answer so that they could determine His approval. However, putting out the fleece is something that is not necessarily used by God today, as He did for Gideon. First you may pray for something that is very obvious, but that answer does not necessarily mean God has directed you. Circumstances would have happened even if you would not have prayed. Second, if you pray for something that would be extremely difficult, i.e., putting out the fleece, and God does it, that may be an answer. But does God lead that way today? Probably not. God speaks through His Word, using the principles of Scriptures to give His people direction. Also God works through the natural laws of the universe; be careful praying against God's laws such as the law of gravity, or laws governing drying and wet objects, or reverse.

I remember praying one time, "God if it doesn't rain today, I will serve you in a particular way." However, that was not a valid request, because even the weatherman showed there were no rain fronts coming through.

THIRD CONFIRMATION: JUDGES 7:1-16, NLT

Gideon blew the trumpet of the Lord, to gather a large army to fight the Midianites. Around 32,000 men gathered at the spring of Harod to form an army. To the north of them in the valley was the Midianites, over 120,000 of them were assembled together.

"The Lord said to Gideon, 'You have too many warriors with you'" (Judges 7:2). The odds of this battle were on the side of the Midianites, over 120,000 people against only 32,000. By today's standard that is around 4 to 1 odds, not very good.

But the Lord said to Gideon, "If I let all of you fight the Midianites, the Israelites will boast to me that they saved themselves by their own strength. Therefore, tell the people, 'Whoever is timid or afraid may leave this mountain and go home'" (Judges 7:2-3). So, when Gideon challenged them, 22,000 of the men left Gideon and went home, leaving only 10,000 willing to fight.

"But the Lord told Gideon 'there were still too many'" (Judges 7:4). Gideon took his warriors down to the water, and there he divided them into two groups. In one group were those who cupped their hands to scoop water to drink. The other group knelt down and drank the water with their mouths. Perhaps the kneeling down with their mouths to the stream was a symbol of worship; some have said that perhaps these people were honoring the God of the water when they were on their faces drinking. But, those who scooped the water with their hands could be on one knee looking across the stream at the opposing army. They were vigilant, ready to fight, they were prepared.

God rejected the 9,700 who were "worshipping" the water. Then God said, "With these 300 men I will rescue you and give you victory over the Midianites" (Judges 7:7). Gideon sent all the rest of the men home.

FOURTH CONFIRMATION: JUDGES 7:9-15, NLT

Even after all that happened, Gideon still had doubts. He was an imperfect man in every sense of the word. "That night the Lord said, 'Get up! Go down into the Midianite camp, for I have given you victory over them!'" (Judges 7:9).

When Gideon went down to the camp God told him to, "Listen to what the Midianites are saying, and you will be greatly encouraged. Then you will be eager to attack." (Judges 7:11).

This night the enemy is described in Scripture as "a swarm of locusts. Their camels were like grains of sand on the seashore—too many to count!" (Judges 7:12).

Do you see a picture of Gideon sneaking to the edge of the enemy camp to spy and listen to what is going on in the Midian camp. "Gideon crept up just as a man was telling his companion about a dream. The man said, 'I had this dream, and in my dream a loaf of barley bread came tumbling down into the Midianite camp. It hit a tent, turned it over, and knocked it flat!'" (Judges 7:13).

"His companion answered, 'Your dream can mean only one thing—God has given Gideon son of Joash, the Israelite, victory over Midian and all its allies!'" (Judges 7:14).

It is interesting that the Hebrew word *Gideon* comes from a Hebrew term for *barley*, i.e., a loaf of barley bread. Perhaps Gideon understood the analogy of this man's dream that he was the barley loaf coming to destroy the enemy.

What happened? "When Gideon heard the dream and its interpretation, he bowed in worship before the Lord" (Judges 7:15). It is interesting that long before the victory when Gideon heard what God was going to do from the mouths of his enemies instead of his own people, he worshiped the Lord. When you know God is going to give you the victory—even before it comes—you should worship Him.

After four confirmations, Gideon finally understands God is going to give a victory through him. When he returns to the camp he shouts, "Get up! For the Lord has given you victory over the Midianite hordes!" (Judges 7:15).

Gideon dividend his men into three groups of 100 men each. It would seem that he would want to keep the 300 men together so they could have courage and victory in numbers, but he divided them. This was *faith-obedience*; Gideon did what God was telling him to do.

Note that their swords stayed in their sheaths, their trust was not in human fighting ability. Their trust was in God Almighty. Each man took a trumpet in one hand and with the other hand, a clay jar with a burning torch in it. The light of the torch was hidden in the clay jar that each man held in one hand. They spread out to surround the camp of the Midianites. Again, a great statement of faith, for each man was separated from a fellow warrior. Each man would have to stand or fight on his own; there was no strength in numbers that night.

It all happened according to timing. "It was just after midnight, after the changing of the guard, when Gideon and the 100 men with him reached the edge of the Midianite camp. Suddenly, they blew the rams' horns and broke their clay jars" (Judges 7:19).

How did they do it? "They held the blazing torches in their left hands and blew the horns in their right hands, then they all shouted, 'A sword for the Lord and for Gideon!'" (Judges 7:20). And where were they? "Each man stood at his position around the camp" (Judges 7:21).

How did God give a great victory? "All the Midianites rushed around in a panic, shouting as they ran to escape...to fight against each other with their swords. Those who were not killed fled to places...far away" (Judges 7:21-22).

dream of one enemy solider had spread throughout the camp and they were fearful of Gideon's coming, but anyway, God gave a great victory.

MOPPING UP

"Gideon sent for the warriors of Naphtali, Asher, and Manasseh, to join in chasing the army of Midian. Gideon also sent messengers throughout the hill country of Ephraim, saying, 'Come down to attack the Midianites. Cut them off at the shallow crossings of the Jordan River at Beth-barah'" (Judges 7:23-24, NLT).

LESSONS TO TAKE AWAY

Remember, your doubts and fears will hold you back from doing what God has commanded you to do. But even then, God has a way of showing His strength and a way to victory.

An imperfect person—Gideon—who comes to God, confesses his weakness to God, and relies in the strength of God and obeys the commands of God, can win a victory. Gideon was the least of his family, his family was the least in their tribe and their tribe was one of the weakness of all in Israel; yet God used Gideon—an imperfect man—to bring about a great victory.

The principle of an organized few can defeat a multitude. We see that 300 men who were determined and obedient won the victory. They put to flight 120,000 soldiers. They did it with three things. First, the enemy saw lights (300 torches) coming from every direction, thinking each light represented a thousand enemy troops coming at them. Second, they heard the ram's horn being sounded, and they knew a trumpet was used as a battle call. Third, they heard the battle cry "A sword for the Lord and Gideon." We don't know if the rumor about the

Chapter 5

THOMAS

A Follower Of Jesus Doubted

JESUS was in the wilderness on the east side of the Jordan River when He received word that His friend Lazarus was sick (John 11:3). The word for sick is *asthenom*, which literally means "without strength." That message didn't appear to be life threatening. Even Jesus commanded, "This sickness is not unto death, but for the glory of God" (John 11:4, KJV). The disciples didn't understand what Jesus meant, because they couldn't see the future as Jesus saw it.

So, "He (Jesus) abode two days in the same plane where He was" (John 11:6, KJV). Apparently Jesus waited two days then told His disciples, "Let us go into Judea again" (John 11:7, KJV). Jesus knew that Lazarus would die, and He would perform a miracle "greater" than healing sickness. Jesus would raise the dead.

The disciples were understandably confused. Why would Jesus remain where He was when He learned Lazarus was not on his deathbed, then risk the dangers of going to Bethany when it was apparent Lazarus was recovering? Later, Jesus resolved their inner confusion, plainly telling His disciples, "Lazarus is dead" (John 11:14). He indicated that somehow His absence during Lazarus' illness was better, because going to him now would strengthen their faith. Even though Lazarus was now dead, Jesus wanted the disciples to accompany Him as He went to him.

Addressing his fellow disciples, Thomas said, "Let us also go, that we may die with Him" (John 11:16). Ironically, this disciple who was first to declare his willingness to follow Jesus to the cross was the last disciple to believe in the reality of Jesus' resurrection from the grave. His attitude toward death may be described as that of doubt and despair. He appears to have been willing to follow Jesus even to death in a somewhat fatalistic way, assuming he was bound to die sooner or later. His attitude at this time, as well as later at the resurrection of Jesus, was anything but faith. Thomas was a doubter—he was imperfect.

Later Thomas interrupted Jesus' discussion in the Upper Room asking the way to the Father (14:5). Apparently Thomas was prepared even then to follow Jesus anywhere. John portrays Thomas as a man of extremes.

In these passages Thomas is both emphatic in his unbelief and his faith.

THOMAS DOUBTS REVEALED

The weeks following Easter Sunday, the disciples marveled at the awesome responsibility that was theirs, that of being witnesses of Jesus' resurrection and communicating to others how they could experience the forgiveness of sins. They knew they would soon be returning to Galilee where Jesus had promised to meet them again, but first there were some loose ends to handle. Thomas had not been with them when they saw Jesus on Easter Sunday evening. Thomas was strong-minded, silent, but also skeptical. He was among the first to whom the disciples told that they had seen Jesus.

Thomas was not with the 10 disciples on Easter Sunday afternoon when they first saw Jesus Christ. Thomas had run away with them, but apparently hid deeper than they. They told Thomas they had seen Jesus. The disciples may have been surprised at Thomas' reluctance to believe their corporate testimony as they reported to him that they had seen the resurrected Jesus. They may have forgotten how reluctant they also had originally been to believe the early reports of the women and Mary Magdalene that Sunday morning. Thomas was just as reluctant to believe, and said, "Unless I see in His hands the print of the nails, and put my finger into the print of the nails, and put my hand into His side, I will not believe" (John 20:25).

To Thomas, his was not an unreasonable request. The disciples themselves claimed they had seen the nail prints when they recognized Jesus that first Sunday afternoon on the day of resurrection (John 20:20).

A week after the Resurrection, on Sunday, April 16, the disciples were again gathered together in the evening. This time Thomas was with the others. Once again, the doors of the room had been bolted as the disciples apparently thought they may still be in danger. No one was really sure what the Jewish leaders were going to do about Jesus' disciples as the conflicting accounts of a stolen body and the resurrection of Jesus were continuing to be reported around town. Then, just as had happened a week earlier, Jesus came and stood in their midst. Again, He greeted His disciples with the familiar "Peace to you!" (John 20:26).

Very soon in this visit, it became clear that Jesus had come primarily for Thomas' benefit. Turning to the doubting disciple, he said, "Reach your finger here, and look at My hands; and reach your hand here, and put it into My side. Do not be unbelieving, but believing" (John 20:27). Just as He had offered the others a close look at the physical evidence of His crucifixion and resurrection from the dead the previous week, Jesus offered Thomas the same opportunity. Thomas had claimed he would not believe until he had put his finger into the print of the nails, and thrust his hand into His side (20:25). The Greek verb translated "put" and "thrust" in this statement is *balo*. The emphatic nature of this verb could be emphasized in both cases with the translation "throw into." Thomas wanted to thrust his finger and hand with great physical energy. Further, in emphasizing his unwillingness to believe, Thomas used a double negative. "You will never make me believe" or "I will not believer...never" (20:25, ELT).

When Thomas saw Jesus standing in the midst of the disciples and heard Him speak, this was enough to produce faith in his heart. He expressed his faith with the confession, "My Lord and my God" (John 20:28).

Jesus responded, "Thomas, because you have seen Me, you have believed. Blessed are those who have not seen and yet believed" (John 20:29). While some

Bible teachers believe this was a rebuke to Thomas for his reluctance to believe, others believe Jesus was commending Thomas for his faith, note the difference implied in the two Greek words used to refer to seeing. The first word *eidon* implies the idea of seeing outwardly, as the act of looking with the eyes. The second word *horao* means to perceive with the mind what the eyes have seen. Jesus told Thomas, "Because you have seen and understand who I am, you have believed. Blessed are those who like you have not examined me by sight and yet believe" (John 20:29, authors translation).

Thomas's response to the presence of Jesus was to confess, "My Lord and my God" (20:28). This is the apex of the Gospel of John because it gives the strongest or highest expression of Old Testament deity (2 Samuel 7:28; 1 Kings 18:39; Psalms 30:2; 35:24; 86:15; 88:1; Jeremiah 38:17; Hosea 2:23). Thomas identified Jesus with both *Jehovah,* the Old Testament "I am," and *Elohim,* the Creator-God. This was Thomas's way of expressing that "Jesus is the Christ, the Son of God" (20:31).

LESSONS TO TAKE AWAY

On the basis of this account in the life of Thomas, he has been branded by Christians as "doubting Thomas." Perhaps in fairness to this disciple it should be remembered that only John appears to have believed in the resurrection before seeing the resurrected Lord. One of the first things Jesus did when He appeared to His disciples was upbraided them (all) for their unbelief (Mark 16:14). Apparently Thomas was typical of the disciples in refusing to believe until he saw. Perhaps in your imperfection, you have doubts. Don't give up, and don't give into your doubts. You can develop great faith (see next paragraph).

Jesus' second appearance to His disciples was similar to His first. This time Thomas was also present.

The major purpose of Jesus' second visit was to bring Thomas from doubt to faith. He did this by inviting Thomas to inspect the marks of the crucifixion using the very language Thomas had earlier used in affirming his unbelief. He concludes with the statement, "and be not faithless, but believing" (20:27, KJV). In the Greek text John uses two closely related words translated "faithless" and "believing." The relationship between the words *apistos* (faithless) and *pistos* (believing) is similar to the English words *unbelieving and believing.* What is the solution to doubts, i.e., the solution for doubting Thomas? It is belief! What is the root cause of imperfection? Unbelief! What is the solution? Belief!

Thomas demonstrates the actuality that some follow Jesus outwardly but have inward doubts. Obviously, all will have doubts as long as they live in human flesh and possess an old nature. However, some have more doubts than others. Of all the eleven believing disciples, did Thomas have more doubts than the others? Was Thomas' doubts emphasized by the gospel writers to show today's readers that the imperfections of Jesus' physical followers is similar to the doubt problem some have today?

The gospels do not emphasize the doubts of other disciples as it does with repeated reference to Thomas' doubts. Perhaps God knew that today's followers of Jesus would have similar problems. If so, we must learn from Thomas' doubts, but not just to stop our expressions of unbelief. We must grow our faith so that we make the same strong statement of faith "My Lord and my God." This is more than an academic expression. Thomas was making a personal belief in Jesus and a personal acceptance of Him as Old Testament deity.

The Bible doesn't tell what happened to Thomas after Pentecost. But early church history records show he eventually went to India to establish and build a strong church. Today there are several Saint Thomas Christian denominations that apparently came from his influence (Wikipedia).

There is another application about doubt that can be learned from Thomas. When doubt resides in the heart (inner person), it becomes evident in the small things we say and do. Note Thomas' apparently innocent statement at Lazarus' sickness that he was willing to go with Jesus to the dangerous area, even if it meant his death (John 11). Also, in the Upper Room, Thomas interrupted Jesus with a doubt expressed in a question. "We have no idea where you are going so how can we know the way?" (John 14:5, NLT). These innocent expressions of doubt reflect Thomas' imperfections. How many innocent expressions of doubt do you express?

Chapter 6

NAOMI

A Bitter Woman Who Lost Everything,
Ended Up A Nourisher

NAOMI, her husband Elimelech, and her two sons Mahlon and Kilion were called, "Ephrathites from Bethlehem-, Judah" (Ruth 1:2). That phrase Ephrathites means upper crust, or when you look at the various levels of society, they were the upper, upper.

A severe famine hit in the Promised Land, including Bethlehem, which has the nickname "house of bread." But because there was little bread, and little of anything else, Elimelech and Naomi looked east from Bethlehem out over the Jordan River Valley. They saw on the hills of Moab lush pastures, and they heard the cities of Moab were prosperous. "When they reached Moab, they settled there" (Ruth 1:2, NLT). The Bible uses an interesting word, *settled*. It means they put roots down, bought a home, and planned to live there permanently. They left the people of God, gave up living in the land of God's promise, ruled by God's law, and where they had access to temple worship. Moab was not only a foreign country; it had a foreign religion and foreign idols that they called god.

At first things went well for Naomi and her family; both of her sons married local women in Moab and life seemed to be going well. But eventually things turned against Naomi and the family. Elimelech died and then both sons died. That left Naomi with two foreign daughters-in-law. "Then Naomi heard in Moab that the Lord had blessed his people in Judah by giving them good crops again" (Ruth 1:6, NLT). So, Naomi planned to return home. She had two problems; her two daughters-in-law were living with her. "With her two daughters-in-law she set out from the place where she had been living, and they took the road that would lead them back to Judah" (Ruth 1:7). At this place Naomi begins to question whether she should or would be able to take these two girls with her. So, she told them, "'Go back to your mothers' homes. And may the Lord reward you for your kindness to your husbands and to me. May the Lord bless you with the security of another marriage.' Then she kissed them good-bye, and they all broke down and wept" (Ruth 1:8-9, NLT).

Naomi told both girls she was too old to have children, i.e., the birth of two sons who could marry these two young girls. Then she used logic, "Would you wait for them to grow up and refuse to marry someone else? No, of course not, my daughters!" (Ruth 1:13, NLT).

Here her bitterness seeps out. She complains, "the Lord himself has raised his fist against me" (Ruth 1:13, NLT).

"Orpah kissed her mother-in-law good-bye. But Ruth clung tightly to Naomi" (Ruth 1:14, NLT). But even then Naomi tried to send her home.

Ruth replies, "Don't ask me to leave you and turn back. Wherever you go, I will go; wherever you live, I will live. Your people will be my people, and your God will be my God" (Ruth 1:16, NLT). Her statement was far more than physical association and protection, this was a statement of Ruth's inner faith; she wanted Naomi's God to be her God.

As they approached Bethlehem, the women of that city were surprised. They questioned if it was really Naomi who was coming back. Probably Naomi had aged, but also circumstances had been hard for her, so her facial features may have changed, gone were here elegant clothes. Her pervious regal attitude was gone.

Naomi told them, "'Don't call me Naomi,' she responded. 'Instead, call me Mara, for the Almighty has made life very bitter for me'" (Ruth 1:20). Naomi was a bitter woman for what had happened to her, and her speech suggested she wanted to be known that way.

There is a principle here: if you turn your back on the plan God has for your life and His presence, you open yourself to the circumstances in the world that can be very bitter and hard. How else would you expect Naomi to look and feel?

WHAT NAOMI DID RIGHT

Naomi recognized God's punishment on her life. "Why call me Naomi when the Lord has caused me to suffer and the Almighty has sent such tragedy upon me?" (Ruth 1:21, NLT). This way Naomi was not looking for sympathy from the people, nor was she expecting the ladies of Bethlehem to receive her as in previous times. She looked at herself honestly and accepted herself for what had happened. Is this true repentance?

It was harvest time, so Ruth asked Naomi, "Let me go out into the harvest fields to pick up the stalks of grain left behind by anyone who is kind enough to let me do it" (Ruth 2:2). This process was called gleaning.

Of course Naomi gave her permission; Ruth was young enough to do the hard work of gathering grain. Perhaps at this time Naomi may not have been able to work hard in the fields, especially under a hot sun.

"And as it happened, she (Ruth) found herself working in a field that belonged to Boaz" (Ruth 2:3, NLT). Ruth did not know who Boaz was, let alone that he was the owner of the field. Since the poor were allowed to go harvest in the fields, Ruth was doing what other vagrants did.

God had commanded, "When you harvest the crops of your land, do not harvest the grain along the edges of your field, and do not pick up what the harvesters drop. Leave it for the poor...I am the Lord your God" (Leviticus 23:22, NLT).

When this commanded is repeated in Leviticus 19:9, it immediately is followed with this admonition, "Ye shall not steal...deal falsely...lie one to another...swear by My name...nor defraud thy neighbor neither rob him" (Deuteronomy 19:11-13, KJV). Therefore, allowing the poor to glean your field was a moral responsibility.

When Naomi found out that Ruth was gleaning in the field of Boaz, her bitterness turned to praise, "'Blessed be he of the Lord, who has not forsaken His kindness to the living and the dead!' And Naomi said to her, 'This man is a relation of ours, one of our close relatives'" (Ruth 2:20,).

Ruth's process of gleaning continued for several days, because the fields were large, and it took time to harvest the grain.

Boaz came to inspect his workers to see how the harvest was coming along. Then he noticed Ruth and asked who she was. Did he notice her beauty, or was it her hard work, or was the Spirit of God beginning a work between the two?

The foreman replied saying she had been working hard all day, and did not take any breaks except for a few minutes to rest in the shelter.

It is then that Boaz told Ruth to stay in his field and glean with his workers. He didn't want her to go to other fields, but work in his fields. Then Boaz told his workers not to treat her roughly and to let her drink from the water barrel when she was thirsty.

Ruth was overwhelmed by this response, she fell at his feet to say, "What have I done to deserve such kindness?" She added, "I am only a foreigner" (Ruth 2:10, NLT).

Boaz knew all about her. He knew what she had done for her mother-in-law and how she left her father and mother in Moab to come make a new life with complete strangers. Then Boaz recognized her faith in the God of Israel, and he blessed her, "May the Lord, the God of Israel, under whose wings you have come to take refuge, reward you fully for what you have done" (Ruth 2:12, NLT).

Later that day Boaz gave her some roasted grain to eat, then he added extra for her to take home to Naomi. After gathering barley all day, Ruth beat out the grain that evening and it filled an entire basket. When she got back home to show it to Naomi, and gave her the roasted grain, the mother-in-law was overwhelmed.

"Where did you gather all this grain today? Where did you work? May the Lord bless the one who helped you!" (Ruth 2:19, NLT).

When Naomi found out the owner of the field was Boaz, she said, "That man is one of our closest relatives, one of our family redeemers" (Ruth 2:20, NLT).

The obligation of a kinsmen redeemer was to redeem or purchase a relative or their property from slavery or bankruptcy (Leviticus 25:48-49). A kinsmen redeemer could also repurchase the property of the relative that had gone into bankruptcy. This sometimes involved marrying the widow of the one who was his relative in order to give them access into the family and its lineage (Deuteronomy 25:5-6).

In the Scriptures this involved redeeming from slavery a brother, uncle, cousin, or other relatives. This could include marrying a sister-in-law who was a widow to bring her into the family.

At this place Naomi saw a path of redemption for both herself and Ruth. "My daughter, it's time that I found a permanent home for you, so that you will be provided for" (Ruth 3:1, NLT).

Naomi told Ruth, "Boaz is a close relative of ours, and he's been very kind by letting you gather grain with his young women. Tonight he will be winnowing barley at the threshing floor. Now do as I tell you—take a bath and put on perfume and dress in your nicest clothes. Then go to the threshing floor, but don't let Boaz see you until he has finished eating and drinking. Be sure to notice where he lies down; then go and uncover his feet and lie down there. He will tell you what to do" (Ruth 3:2-4, NLT).

That is exactly the way events happened that evening. Usually at the end of a harvest there was a great feast, with singing, dancing and merriment. Then the owner would usually slept next to his harvest to guard its safety. That night as he slept, Ruth came to assume the role of a servant. A servant would lay at the feet of the master, and in the cold night would put the mater's cold feet on the servant to keep the master warm. Is this what happened?

"Around midnight Boaz suddenly woke up and turned over. He was surprised to find a woman lying at his feet! 'Who are you?' he asked" (Ruth 3:8-9, NLT).

Ruth's response was her invitation for him to exercise his role as kinsmen redeemer over her family rights that she had received from Naomi's son, i.e., Ruth's husband. She said, "I am your servant Ruth,... spread the corner of your covering over me, for you are my family redeemer" (Ruth 3:9, NLT).

Boaz assured her that everything would be done right. He said he would go into town the next day and do what was necessary. He said, "Everyone in town knows you are a virtuous woman. But while it is true that I am one of your family redeemers, there is another man who is more closely related to you than I am" (Ruth 3:11-12, NLT). Boaz counseled her to stay the night and he would take care of the matter the following morning.

Early in the morning Ruth got up and before it was light Boaz placed several scoops of grain into her coat and sent her home.

"Ruth told Naomi everything Boaz had done for her, and she added, 'He gave me these six scoops of barley and said, "Don't go back to your mother-in-law empty-handed"'" Ruth 3:16-17, NLT).

When Ruth revealed her identity to Boaz, "I am your handmaid," she urged Boaz to spread his robe over her—thus becoming her protector. Also this was an act of *goal*, meaning to buy her land and redeem it out of bankruptcy.

The land of Elimelech at his death went to the husband of Ruth, but when he died technically the bankrupt land belonged to her. Apparently, because Elimelech was out of the country, while they were gone the land was probably sold at auction. Someone else now owned it.

Boaz told Ruth that he could not redeem the land because there was another man in town who was a closer relative to Naomi's husband than him. He had more right to the land than Boaz.

The next morning Boaz went to the town gate, the site for legal transactions in Judah. He found Naomi's kinsmen, the man is not named in the Bible, who had legal rights to redeem the property that was in bankruptcy because the family had been in Moab.

Boaz asked the kinsman if he wished to buy Naomi's land, because she could not buy it herself. Boaz wanted the land to stay in the family and not leave the clan. When the man replied he would redeem it, then Boaz told him he also had to marry Ruth, because Naomi's son had been married to Ruth. But her husband was dead. In other words, the property in question should have been inherited by the child of Ruth.

This changed the circumstances for the man in the marketplace. He withdrew his offer to buy the land because of some reason, we don't know what the reason was.

So now the property was open for Boaz to purchase. To seal the deal in those days, a sandal was exchanged between the two men, this was a legal custom in those days. Probably the sandal was a symbol of walking the boundaries of the land in question. That would be similar to a handshake in today's terminology. In those days exchanging the sandal sealed the deal.

Back in Bethlehem everyone seemed to be pleased at the turn of events. The townswomen all at once began to praise Ruth, who had been a foreigner to them. They compared her to the great mothers of Israel, who also were foreigners before coming into the Hebrew family, i.e., Rachel and Leah (Ruth 4:11).

The story ends with Ruth being lifted out of obscurity and poverty to marry a godly rich man who was well thought of in the community and a property owner.

Although Naomi's natural hope was gone when she left Moab, now she lived again in the life of her grandson Obed, who was Ruth's firstborn son. The Bible pictures Obed being cared for by Grandma Naomi. Their relation was so cordial, Ruth was better to Naomi than seven sons (Ruth 4:15).

The family that looked like it was going to be destroyed and pass out of existence is restored and included in the genealogy of the coming Messiah. Baby Obed lived to become the father of Jesse, who was the father of the great King David. In essence, Ruth's son became the great-grandfather to David, the greatest king of all.

LESSONS TO TAKE AWAY

God can overlook the mistakes and sins of your youth and use you greatly in your old age. Naomi who began as a wealthy aristocrat in Bethlehem, lost everything. But through the transition and intervention of God, her daughter-in-law Ruth married Boaz. Naomi was given the responsibly of raising the grandfather of King David.

It is easy to list Naomi's mistakes; like all of God's children, she was imperfect. But we remember Naomi because God used her in spite of her mistakes and imperfections. God used her for His glory.

Naomi is an illustration of God giving a second chance. Naomi was given a second chance to raise a son after she lost both of her sons because of disobedience. Now in the protection of Boaz's family, she raised Obed as a servant of God.

Chapter 7

SAMSON

Wrongly Trusted His Own Strength

THE Book of Judges tells of seven judges, each used of God to deliver different tribes of Israel from persecution and/or enslavement by the warring nations that occupied the Promised Land after Joshua began to drive them out of the land. But those nations/tribes that were not completely cleared out of the Promised Land. They later regained strength and turned against God's people. Just as each judge was identified with one tribe, or a few tribes, so God used Samson the judge from the tribe of Dan to fight against the Philistines.

"Again the children of Israel did evil in the sight of the Lord, and the Lord delivered them into the hand of the Philistines for forty years" (Judges 13:1). Among the enemies of Israel in the Old Testament, the Philistines were certainly among the most powerful. When God raised up Samson as a judge to deal with the oppression of the Philistines, he was commissioned only to "begin to deliver Israel out of the hand of the Philistines" (v. 5). It would not be until much later that David would finish what Samson had begun.

Dan was among the first tribes to lose territory to the Philistines. By the time the Angel of the Lord first appeared to the wife of Manoah, much of the tribe of Dan had already migrated to the south of the Promised Land and settled in a kind of refugee camp situated between Zorah and Eshtaol (13:25). This tribe, which was not strong enough to defend its own territory, was not the likely place to look for a champion like Samson, to deliver Israel, "but God has chosen the foolish things of the world to put to shame the wise; and God has chosen the weak things of the world to put to shame the things which are mighty" (1 Corinthians 1:27). Also today, God chooses imperfect people to do His work, just as He chose imperfect Samson as a judge to begin delivering Israel from the Philistines.

THE WIFE OF MANOAH —
JUDGES 13:1-25

(1123 B.C.)

The life of Samson can be outlined in relationship to the four women who dominated his life to some degree. The first of these was his mother whose name is never named in Scripture but described only as the wife of Manoah. She was barren in the culture of the Near East, where not bearing children was generally viewed as an evidence of the displeasure of God. "And the Angel of the Lord appeared to the woman and said to her, 'Indeed now, you are barren and have borne no children, but you shall conceive and bear a son'" (Judges 13:3).

The wife of Manoah was instructed to abstain from wine, strong drink, and foods classified as unclean in the Law. The reason for this action on her part was that the son was to be "a Nazarite to God from the womb" (v. 5). Under the Law, there was a provision made for a Nazarite, he dedicated himself to a particular work for God. As a Nazarite, he was to demonstrate his commitment to God by observing three conditions. Some Nazarites are dedicated to God from the womb (cf. also 1 Samuel 1:11; Luke 1:15).

Conditions of the Nazarite Vow

1. Not eat or touch the unclean
2. Not drink wine or strong drink
3. No razor to cur his hair

The Angel of the Lord spoke to the wife of Manoah, but she failed to recognize this as a Christophany or preincarnate appearance of Christ. Still, she was aware the man who spoke with her was unusual. She told her husband, describing Him as "a man of God." "His countenance was like the countenance of the Angel of God, very awesome" (Judges 13:6). She told her husband their son was destined as "a Nazarite to God from the womb to the day of his death" (v. 7).

Manoah demonstrated his deep faith in God by requesting from God a second visitation of this "Man of God," so He would "teach us what we shall do for the child who will be born" (v. 8). He realized his great responsibility as the father of a very special son, "And God listened to the voice of Manoah" (v. 9).

The second time the Angel of the Lord appeared to the wife of Manoah, she was sitting alone in a field. Knowing her husband wanted to meet this person, she quickly ran to get him. When Manoah arrived, the Angel of the Lord confirmed He was the One who had appeared to Manoah's wife earlier. The earlier message was repeated and emphasized. When Manoah realized he was talking with the Angel of the Lord, he offered to prepare a kid and serve it as a meal. The Angel said he would not eat the food but rather encouraged Manoah to offer it as a burnt offering unto the Lord. When Manoah asked the Angel His name, he was told it was Secret or Wonderful, one of the distinct titles of Christ in the Scriptures (cf. Isaiah 9:6).

When Manoah prepared his burnt offering and a meal offering and placed it on a rock, "the Angel of the Lord ascended in the flame of the altar" (Judges 13:20). While Manoah felt certain he would die, having seen God, his wife pointed out that the acceptance of the sacrifice by the Lord suggested their lives would be preserved.

"So the woman bore a son and called his name Samson" (v. 24). The name Samson, or *shimshon* as it is in Hebrew, means "sunny." Samson was endued with great strength by the Spirit of the Lord. Yet this physically strong man of God had a glaring weakness that would eventually destroy him. He failed to learn to discipline himself in controlling his desires toward women. Samson was imperfect in this area.

THE WOMAN OF TIMNAH—JUDGES 14:1-15:20

(1104 B.C.)

Samson's lack of self-discipline first became evident in his choice of a bride from among the Philistines. Under the Law, Israel had been specifically instructed not to intermarry with those of other nations who worshiped other gods. This in itself should have prevented Samson from selecting a Philistine bride. Also, Samson must have known by this time he had been raised up by God to begin delivering Israel from the Philistines. Having a Philistine wife would certainly compromise his ability to do what he knew God wanted him to do.

When Samson told his parents he wanted to take the Philistine as his bride, they naturally objected, suggesting that he find a wife from among his own people. But Samson was insistent and his father finally consented to make the necessary arrangements. What Samson failed to tell his parents was that he also had an alternative motive in marrying the Philistine woman. "He was seeking an occasion against the Philistines" (Judges 14:4).

As Samson made his way to Timnah to meet with his bride-to-be, he was attacked by a young lion in the vineyards of Timnah. As a Nazarite, Samson was not to eat or drink of the fruit of the vine. That being the case, why was Samson in the vineyard? The most probable explanation was that Samson was on the verge of violating one of the conditions of his Nazarite vow. Could it be the lion may have been an interruption sent by God to prevent him from falling into sin. But Samson, who could conquer massive Philistine warriors, could not control himself.

Violations of the Nazarite Vow

1. Touched dead lion/ate unclean honey
2. Attended a drinking fest
3. Cut his hair

When Samson returned to the Philistine city to take the woman to be his wife, "he turned aside to see the carcass of the lion" (v. 8). There he discovered a swarm of bees were using the decaying carcass of the lion as a hive and it was filled with honey. He took some of the unclean honey and ate it. Though he shared it with his parents, he was careful not to tell them where he had found it, just as he had avoided telling them he had killed the lion in the vineyard originally. Samson must have known his parents would object to his compromise of his Nazarite vows.

It was customary for the Philistines to conduct a seven-day drinking feast as part of a marriage. Samson was the host of such a feast. The couple was married early in the week-long celebration, but the marriage was not consummated until the groom took his bride home on the last night of the feast. Samson used the occasion of the feast to make a wager with the thirty Philistine men who gathered at the feast. If they could solve a riddle, he would give each of them a new garment. But if they failed, it was they who were to give him the new garments. The riddle was expressed by Samson, "Out of the eater came something to eat, and out of the strong came something sweet" (v. 14). Despite their efforts, the Philistines were unable to solve the riddle during the next three days.

When the Philistines realized they could not solve the riddle, they threatened Samson's wife to tell them the riddle or be burned alive with her father in her father's house. Rather than telling her husband of the threat and letting him defend her, she chose to manipulate him into revealing the secret of the riddle.

Samson's wife "wept on him the seven days while the feast lasted" (14:17). She accused Samson of not loving her and keeping secrets from her. Finally, as the result of her constant nagging, he told her the secret of the riddle, "then she explained the riddle to the sons of her people" (v. 17). The men were able to win the wager, but Samson was not deceived. He knew how they had learned the answer. He paid off his debt by making a quick trip to Ashkelon and killing thirty Philistines. The garments of his victims were then given to the men of the city. In his anger, Samson returned to his father's house without his bride. To save the forsaken bride any undue embarrassment, she was given in marriage to the "best man" as was the custom of those days.

Sometime later, Samson cooled off enough to realize he had forgotten to bring his bride home. He returned to Timnah to collect her only to learn her father had married her off to the best man. The father offered the girl's younger sister as a substitute wife for Samson, arguing she was prettier than the daughter Samson had intended to marry. But Samson refused. As he left the city, he caught 300 foxes and tied them together in pairs. He then attached torches to their tails and sent them running wild through the fields, vineyards, and orchards of the city. The crops, vineyards, and olive groves were all destroyed by fire. When the men of the city learned Samson was the cause of this catastrophe, they burned his wife and father-in-law. Samson attacked a number of Philistines, "he attacked them hip and thigh with a great slaughter" (15:8).

When the Philistines learned Samson was living at the top of the rock of Etam, they came against Judah in battle. Eager to avoid a military conflict with the Philistines, the men of Judah sought to negotiate a peace treaty with the Philistines. The terms to which they agreed involved turning Samson over to the Philistines bound. Samson agreed to let the men of Judah bind him and turn him over to the Philistines, provided they agreed not to fall on him themselves. They bound him in two new cords and took him to them.

The Philistines were overjoyed when they saw their enemy bound. But they did not realize how strong Samson could be when endued with the power of the Holy Spirit. As they shouted, "against him," Samson broke the cords and began fighting against the Philistines. Not having a weapon, "he found a fresh jawbone of a donkey, reached out his hand and took it, and killed a thousand men with it" (v. 15). The victory Samson won on that occasion resulted in the renaming of the place *Ramath Lehi* meaning "the hill of the jawbone." "And he judged Israel twenty years in the days of the Philistines" (v. 20).

THE HARLOT OF GAZA— JUDGES 16:1-3

For twenty years, Samson judged Israel and apparently controlled his own desires to some extent. Toward the end of that period, he was again attracted physically by a Philistine woman. He made a trip to Gaza to spend a night with a prostitute in that city. When the men of the city learned he was there, they set an ambush intending to kill him as he left the city the next morning.

About midnight, Samson got up and left the harlot. Some writers have suggested Samson may have begun to realize the error of his way and decided to leave before he compromised himself any further. It was customary for cities to lock their gates at night as part of the defense of the city. When Samson came to the locked gate, he lifted them on his shoulders and carried them thirty-eight miles toward the city of Hebron. The men who sat in ambush waiting for Samson were undoubtedly stunned as they saw this man lift approximately 4,000 pounds (two tons) and carry them off. None of them made any effort to attack Samson as he left the city.

DELILAH OF SOREK—JUDGES 16:4-31

(1084 B.C.)

The fourth woman influencing Samson was Delilah of Sorek, near Gaza. Though Delilah herself is never identified as a Philistine, she was certainly in league with the Philistines. When the five lords of the Philistines learned of Samson's interest in Delilah, they offered to each pay her 11,000 pieces of silver if she could uncover the secret of his strength. Even by contemporary standards, that amounts to a small fortune. The immensity of this reward is perhaps best illustrated when it is realized Judas Iscariot betrayed Jesus for only 30 pieces of silver. Delilah agreed to try to learn the secret of his strength in exchange for the reward.

Deadly Lover's Game

1. Bind with bow strings
2. Bind with new ropes
3. Weave my hair
4. Cut my hair

Delilah sought to learn the secret of Samson's strength by playing a "deadly lover's game." After she had set Samson at ease, she appealed to him to reveal the secret of his strength. Samson played along with the game, giving her false answers. But each time he did so, he was getting closer to revealing the true source of his strength. What he did not realize was that Delilah had men waiting to take him as soon as the true secret of his strength was revealed. Only when Delilah was convinced she knew the source of his strength did she call the lords of the Philistines to collect her reward.

When Delilah knew the strength of Samson could be destroyed if his hair was cut, she caused him to sleep on her lap. While he slept, she had a man cut the seven braids of Samson's hair. Then she woke him with the now familiar words, "The Philistines are upon you" (Judges 16:9, 12, 14, 20). He assumed he could shake off everything and fight as he had done before. Tragically the Scripture records, "but he did not know that the Lord had departed from him" (v. 20). The strong man of Israel was without his strength. He would suffer the consequences of his sin. He was bound and blinded by the enemy and taken to the prison where he would do the work of a woman grinding out grain. In a sudden reversal of circumstances, the former victories of Samson now came back to haunt him in his greatest defeat.

The Consequence of Sin (16:21)

1. Blinding
2. Binding
3. Grinding

THE BESETTING SIN IS AVENGED

Samson was not destined to end his life in the service of the Philistine god Dagon but rather in the service of the Lord God of Israel. After Samson became a prisoner, his hair began to grow again. He would have one more opportunity to use his God-given strength in accordance with the purpose God had established for his life.

The Philistines were eager to celebrate their great victory over Samson and attribute it to their god Dagon. They gathered their people to the temple of Dagon and offered sacrifices to their god and feasted together. As the celebration continued, a decision was made to bring Samson to the temple as a form of entertainment. He was taken from the prison and brought into the temple where everyone could see him.

The temple of Dagon was a massive two-tiered structure which rested on a series of pillars for support. While there were a number of pillars between the two floors of the temple, the weight of the second floor was supported primarily by the corner pillars. Samson had a boy who was acting as his guide take him to these support pillars in preparation for his final battle with the Philistines. Resting against those pillars, Samson prayed one last time. "O Lord God, remember me, I pray! Strengthen me, I pray, just this once, O God, that I may with one blow take vengeance on the Philistines for my two eyes!" (Judges 16:28) Realizing this final battle would cost him his life, he added, "Let me die with the Philistines!" (v. 30)

With one last demonstration of the immense strength God had given him, Samson moved the support pillars from their place, causing the roof of the building to collapse and killing those who were in the temple of Dagon. While there is no record of the total number of people killed in the destruction of the temple of Dagon, there were about 3,000 men and women on the roof alone at the time of the collapse. "So the dead that he killed at his death were more than he had killed in his life" (v. 30).

LESSON TO TAKE AWAY

Of all the people God used, Samson might have been the most imperfect of them all. He constantly returned to his "besetting sin," i.e., the physical strong man was made captive by the attraction of women (think of a woman as the weaker sex, yet could exercise power over a man). The Bible describes the continuous influence of a practical sin that trips up the believer is a *besetting sin*. "Lay aside every weight and the sin which doth so easily beset us, let us run...the race...looking to Jesus" (Hebrews 12:1-2, KJV). Apparently the appearance of Jesus as a Christophany at his birth, was not to taught to Samson. He didn't rely on that strength when he could have used it.

Another lesson imperfect Samson didn't learn, when you are burned with fire, don't go back to play with it or you might be burned again, or, even worst. Samson had more than one negative experience with women, but he did not learn. Also, he used three "excuses" to mislead Delilah and didn't learn that she was trying to discover the secret of his strength. While the secret of his strength was not known, remember, the One who gave Samson the strength in the first place, was the one called secret. "And the angel of the Lord said, 'Why askest thou thus after my name, seeing it is secret?'" (Judges 13:18, KJV).

Chapter 8

SOLOMON
The World's Wisest Made Bad Choices

WHEN you think about the best, you think of those who do the most for God, or those who accomplish the most for God, or those who are recognized by many people for what they do for God. Somehow those qualities make us think a certain person is the best of all persons. However, when you look at Solomon, here is a man who one of the wisest men in the world; he wrote three books in the Bible, plus two psalms; he built one of the most magnificent edifices called Solomon's Temple; he ruled in peace and did not have a major war during his reign; he ruled more land for God than any other, i.e., from Euphrates River all the way to Egypt; he protected people with forts, towers and armies; and not only that, he was one of the wealthiest men in the world. As a matter of fact, a recent internet article disclosed he is one of the 20th wealthiest persons of all history. Solomon was one of the greatest, and one of the wisest man in the world, yet he was imperfect. Solomon made some bad choices.

It is often said that great leaders have a dream, and the power of that dream gives them focus in life, strength to endure all temptations and barriers, and fortitude to win the battle. Solomon had a dream where God spoke to him, and that too was the defining experience in his life.

THE DREAM: 1 KINGS 3 AND 10, NLT

"Solomon loved the Lord and followed all the decrees of his father, David, except that Solomon, too, offered sacrifices and burned incense at the local places of worship. The most important of these places of worship was at Gibeon, so the king went there and sacrificed 1,000 burnt offerings. That night the Lord appeared to Solomon in a dream, and God said, 'What do you want? Ask, and I will give it to you!'" (1 Kings 3:3-5).

Solomon answered, "I am like a little child who doesn't know his way around. And here I am in the midst of your own chosen people, a nation so great and numerous they cannot be counted! Give me an understanding heart so that I can govern your people well and know the difference between right and wrong" (1 Kings 3:7-9).

"The Lord was pleased that Solomon had asked for wisdom. So God replied, 'Because you have asked for wisdom in governing my people with justice and have not asked for a long life or wealth or the death of your enemies— I will give you what you asked for!'" (1 Kings 3:10-12).

But then God added, "I will also give you what you did not ask for—riches and fame! No other king in all the world will be compared to you for the rest of your life! And if you follow me and obey my decrees and my commands as your father, David, did, I will give you a long life" (1 Kings 3:13-14).

To show the greatness of Solomon, after he woke up from the dream where God spoke to him, he returned to Jerusalem to stand before the Ark of the covenant—God's presence—and there he sacrificed burnt offerings and peace offerings. He was thankful to God for answering his prayer and showed gratitude with sacrifices. What more could you ask for in a great leader?

Perhaps the greatest testimony of the wisdom of Solomon was heard from the mouth of the Queen of Sheba, i.e., Ethiopia. She testified, "I believed not... until I came and saw...the whole half was not told me, thy wisdom and property exccedeth your fame" (1 Kings 10:7, KJV).

The intent of the Queen of Sheba, "She came to test him with hard questions" (1 Kings 10:1). As they met and talked, the Bible describes, "She talked with him about everything she had on her mind. Solomon had answers for all her questions; nothing was too hard for the king to explain to her" (1 Kings 10:2-3). The Queen of Sheba was also, "amazed at the food on his tables, the organization of his officials and their splendid clothing, the cup-bearers, and the burnt offerings Solomon made at the Temple of the Lord" (1 Kings 10:5).

"Then she gave the king a gift of 9,000 pounds of gold, great quantities of spices, and precious jewels. Never again were so many spices brought in as those the Queen of Sheba gave to King Solomon" (1 Kings 10:10).

And how rich was Solomon? "Each year Solomon received about 25 tons of gold" (1 Kings 10:14). To show off his wealth, "King Solomon made 200 large shields of hammered gold, each weighing more than fifteen pounds. He also made 300 smaller shields of hammered gold, each weighing nearly four pounds" (1 Kings 10:16-17).

SOLOMON'S TEMPLE

The crowning achievement of King Solomon was the erection of God's magnificent temple on Mount Zion in Jerusalem, i.e., afterwards called Solomon's Temple. Solomon's father David had wanted to build the great temple, but because he was a man of war who had shed blood (1 Chronicles 28:3), he was not permitted to build the temple. But David gathered the resources necessary to build the temple.

Its size was enormous. The inside celling was 180 feet long, 90 feet wide, and 50 feet high. Actually, the highest point of the temple was 120 cubits or about 20 stories tall, i.e., 207 feet.

Solomon spared no expenses for building this beautiful temple. He ordered great quantities of cedar from King Hiram of Tyre (Lebanon) (1 Kings 5:6). He had huge blocks of the choicest stone quarried and brought to Jerusalem.

Solomon was a master at delegation, he employed architects, plus 3,600 foremen to supervise the work (1 Kings 5:13-17).

The events of the temple's dedication are described in 2 Chronicles 6:1-42. The dedication included a tremendous amount of animal sacrifices including 22,000 bulls and 120,000 sheep. These sacrifices were offered outside the temple and in the middle court of the temple because the altar inside the temple despite its extensive dimensions was not big enough for that many sacrifices on that day. However the celebration lasted eight days and was attended by a great assembly and subsequent feast of tabernacles extended the whole celebration to 14 days. Then the people were sent to their homes.

After the dedication, God again spoke to Solomon in a dream to say He would hear his prayers, and would continue to hear the prayers of the people and bless the nations. God gave four ways in 2 Chronicles 7:14 whereby they could continue receiving the blessing of God. First, humility, second, prayer, third, seek His face, and fourth turn from their wicked ways. However, God warned if the people turned aside, forsook His commandments, and worshiped other gods, then He would abandon them and the temple.

When the Ark of the Covenant, a symbol of the presence of God, was brought into the temple, "At that moment a thick cloud filled the Temple of the Lord. The priests could not continue their service because of the cloud, for the glorious presence of the Lord filled the Temple of God" (2 Chronicles 5:13-14, NLT).

Then Solomon stood on the large bronze platform that had been constructed for the occasion, "'O Lord, You have said that You would live in a thick cloud of darkness. Now I have built a glorious Temple for You, a place where You can live forever!' Then the king turned around to the entire community of Israel standing before him and gave this blessing: 'Praise the Lord, the God of Israel, who has kept the

promise he made to my father, David'" (2 Chronicles 6:1-4, NLT).

WRITINGS OF SOLOMON

Solomon wrote *The Song of Solomon* with the passion of his first love emphasizing his love for a shepherd girl. Young Solomon met her when he served as a shepherd in one of his father's farms. Solomon's second book *Proverbs* emphasized what he used in building the kingdom of Israel—wisdom, godly leadership, and the Word of God. He continually emphasizes and describes wisdom with principles and practical slogans on how to live and serve God. He also describes the fool who destroyed himself and those who followed his advice or example.

Solomon's third book *Ecclesiastes* was written in his old age after his many successes in his pursuits of life. It also includes his failures with his many women, lack of contentment with luxury, and his boredom with power and authority. After everything had been said in *Ecclesiastes,* his final words are, "Here now is my final conclusion: Fear God and obey his commands, for this is everyone's duty. God will judge us for everything we do, including every secret thing, whether good or bad" (Ecclesiastes 12:13-14, NLT).

SOLOMON'S RULE

Solomon ruled in peace, whereas his father David had been a man of war conquering lands and nations. Solomon made peace with all his neighboring nations by marrying the daughters of the various leaders. "Throughout the lifetime of Solomon, all of Judah and Israel lived in peace and safety; and each family had its own home and garden" (1 Kings 4:25, LB).

Solomon ruled an area larger than the Holy Land, larger than any other Jewish king before him or after. "Israel and Judah were a wealthy, populous, contented nation at this time. King Solomon ruled the whole area from the Euphrates River...down to the borders of Egypt. The conquered peoples...sent taxes to Solomon and continued to serve him throughout his lifetime" (1 Kings 4:20-21, LB).

But it wasn't just the nation he improved—he lifted the standard of living for all of his people. The people both under David and King Solomon were simple farmers. A yearly salary for a Levite minister before King David was 10 shekels (Judges 17:10), however Solomon paid a vineyard keeper 600 shekels (Song of Solomon 8:11).

How would you describe Solomon's accomplishments? "He built to his heart's desire in Jerusalem and Lebanon and throughout the entire realm" (2 Chronicles 8:6, LB).

When you speak about the wealth of Solomon, "Each year Solomon received gold worth a quarter of a billion dollars" (1 Kings 10:14, LB). "All of King Solomon's cups were of solid gold...silver wasn't used because it wasn't considered to be of much value!" (1 Kings 10:21, LB).

SOLOMON'S FUTILITY

The book of Ecclesiastes demonstrates Solomon's futility of life. "I also tried to find meaning by building huge homes for myself and by planting beautiful vineyards ... filling them with all kinds of fruit trees. I built reservoirs to collect the water to irrigate my many flourishing groves...I also owned large herds and flocks, more than any of the kings who had lived in Jerusalem before me. I collected great sums of silver and gold...I hired wonderful singers, both men and women, and had many beautiful concubines. I

had everything a man could desire!" (Ecclesiastes 2:4-8, NLT).

Solomon lived the extension of his dreams, everything he wished for he had, everything he wanted he acquired, until he ran out of dreams. "Anything I wanted, I would take. I denied myself no pleasure" (Ecclesiastes 2:10). What was his conclusion? "It was all so meaningless—like chasing the wind. There was nothing really worthwhile anywhere." (Ecclesiastes 2:11).

SOLOMON'S DOWNFALL: 1 KINGS 11, NLT

It is widely reported that Solomon had 700 wives and 300 concubines...that is 1,000 women. The Bible describes it, "Now King Solomon loved many foreign women" (1 Kings 11:1). "Besides Pharaoh's daughter, he married women from Moab, Ammon, Edom, Sidon, and from among the Hittites. The Lord had clearly instructed the people of Israel, 'You must not marry them, because they will turn your hearts to their gods.' Yet Solomon insisted on loving them anyway...in fact, they did turn his heart away from the Lord" (1 Kings 11:2-3).

While Solomon accomplished much in the beginning of his kingdom, even in his middle age he still was doing much for God, "In Solomon's old age, they turned his heart to worship other gods instead of being completely faithful to the Lord his God, as his father, David, had been. Solomon worshiped Ashtoreth, the goddess of the Sidonians, and Molech, the detestable god of the Ammonites. In this way, Solomon did what was evil in the Lord's sight; he refused to follow the Lord completely, as his father, David, had done" (1 Kings 11:4-6).

Here is insight into to Solomon's life that most people miss. "The Lord was very angry with Solomon, for his heart had turned away from the Lord, the God of Israel, who had appeared to him twice. He had warned Solomon specifically about worshiping other gods, but Solomon did not listen to the Lord's command. So now the Lord said to him, 'Since you have not kept my covenant and have disobeyed my decrees, I will surely tear the kingdom away from you and give it to one of your servants'" (1 Kings 11:9-11).

God even predicted that the man who would divide the kingdom would not do it in his lifetime, but God promised to take the kingdom away from his son. Then God promised that one tribe would be governed by his son for David's sake. "But for the sake of your father, David, I will not do this while you are still alive. I will take the kingdom away from your son. And even so, I will not take away the entire kingdom; I will let him be king of one tribe, for the sake of my servant David and for the sake of Jerusalem, my chosen city" (1 Kings 11:12-13).

LESSONS TO TAKE AWAY

Just because God used you at a young age does not guarantee your usefulness in your middle age or even into old age. Look at the example of Solomon who was used greatly as a young man and even into his middle age. But Solomon's sin and foolish decisions caused him to lose favor with God as an old man.

Be careful about the good things you pray for; they can dilute your faith and/or take away your passion for God. Solomon prayed for wisdom, and God gave it to him. But with all of his wisdom, he made foolish choices about women. Also we can question his ostentatious display of wealth, gold, and all the luxuries he had. Remember, gold—money— is always a tool to be used, it is never the ultimate aim in life. If you plan to use your gold or money for God's glory and to carry out the Great Commission, God can and will use you.

The most valuable things in life do not involve money, the most valuable things in life are family, integrity, honor and dignity. These are the things that money cannot buy. Jesus said, "Wherever your treasure is, there the desires of your heart will also be." (Matthew 6:21, NLT). The desires of your heart are more important than your money. It reveals who you really are, what you want in life, and where you are going. Your desires will ultimately tell who you will be in old age.

Chapter 9

RICH YOUNG RULER
A Wealthy Man Learned Value

AMONG those who approached Jesus was a man simply known as the Rich Young Ruler. He had been impressed with Jesus and wanted to follow Him. He called Jesus, "good Teacher" (Luke 18:18). He asked what the conditions were to obtain eternal life. Jesus reminded the young man only God is good and only by keeping His commandments could he enter into eternal life.

This Rich Young Ruler insisted he had kept all the commandments from his youth and wanted to know what he lacked.

Jesus responded, "If you want to be perfect, go, sell what you have and give to the poor, and you will have treasure in heaven; and come, follow Me" (Matthew 19:21). Jesus' advice to this man is puzzling because He did not give this requirement to others, i.e., to give up their possessions to become His disciples.

Some Bible teachers believe Jesus added this requirement here because He knew the Rich Young Ruler was wrapped up in his money and would not be able to serve both God and riches.

According to an early church tradition, the Rich Young Ruler was a Levite from Cyprus named Joses but was nicknamed Barnabas by the apostles in the early days of the church. (Acts 5:36-37). If this was the case, the young ruler's possessions were illegal for a Levite. They were the priestly tribe of Israel, and God did not allow them to own land (Numbers 18:20-21; Deuteronomy 10:8-9). They were to live off the tithes and offerings that other Israelites donated at the temple. Apparently, Barnabas was born into the priestly line but had broken the requirements for Levites. Later, when Barnabas was converted, he sold his land and gave the money to the apostles to be distributed as they saw fit (Acts 4:37). Barnabas was doing what Jesus asked the Rich Young Ruler to do.

But on this occasion, the Rich Young Ruler "went away sorrowful, for he had great possessions" (Matthew 19:22). As the Rich Young Ruler left, Jesus said, "Assuredly, I say to you that it is hard for a rich man to enter the kingdom of heaven. And again I say to you, it is easier for a camel to go through the eye of a needle than for a rich man to enter the kingdom of God" (Matthew 19:23-24). The disciples would no doubt be confused as they considered this statement and reflected on the conversation they had just witnessed between Jesus and the Rich Young Ruler. Jews generally believed that riches were an evidence of God's blessing. Now Jesus seemed to be indicating riches would prevent a person from experiencing the ultimate blessing of God, that of entering into the kingdom. "Who then can be saved?" they wondered. Jesus reminded His disciples, "With men this is impossible, but with God all things are possible" (Matthew 19:26).

But there is another fact. The gospel of Mark adds, "Jesus looking at him, loved him" (Mark 10:21). Jesus had deep sympathy for this "Levite" who had good intentions of being Jesus' disciple. The heavenly Father used the love of His Son to touch his life. So, Barnabas sold all and followed Jesus. Obviously this imperfect Levite was eventually used by God.

"Now the multitude of those who believed were of one heart and one soul; neither did anyone say that any of the things he possessed was his own...a converted Levite named Joses with the nickname Barnabas, which means 'son of encouragement,' sold his land and his home in Cyprus and gave the money to the apostles to be distributed to meet the needs of others" (Acts 4:32, 36-37, expanded).

The church in Antioch, Syria, was the first church to begin making the transition from being predominantly Jewish in character to becoming predominantly Gentile in its outlook. The change did not pass unnoticed by the church in Jerusalem. When they heard what was taking place, they determined to send someone to be certain the Antioch church had not gone too far. Also, the church's location in a crucial city meant its influence could be empire-wide. Barnabas was selected for the job, probably because he shared common Cypriot roots with some of those who were instrumental in establishing the church at Antioch.

Barnabas had already earned a reputation for being an "encourager." He could find potential in people and build them up. He had been a source of encouragement to the apostles in the early days of the church in Jerusalem. Barnabas was one of the first to accept Saul of Tarsus after he had been converted (Acts 9:26-27).

So, as Barnabas traveled north to Antioch, it was only natural for him to remember he had owned property in Cyprus but sold it. It was a road Barnabas had previously travel to visit his land holdings in Cyprus. Arriving in Antioch, he no doubt recognized some things that were being done differently in this predominantly Gentile church. But he rejoiced in the evidences he saw of God's grace at work in their midst "and encouraged them all that with purpose of heart they should continue with the Lord" (Acts 11:23). Wasn't his gift encouragement?

Barnabas was a good man who ministered faithfully in the power of the Holy Spirit and God used his ability for a great ministry. As he preached in the church at Antioch, "A great many people were added to the Lord" (Acts 11:24). Barnabas quickly realized that one of the problems confronting this church was the people's cultural background. In Jerusalem, most converts understood the Old Testament Scriptures well and had a foundation upon which they could build their personal relationship with God. Here in Antioch, most new converts did not have an Old Testament background. This church needed a gifted teacher who could instruct these Gentile converts in their new faith. As a Levite, Barnabas was no doubt capable of performing this ministry, but as he thought about the situation, he remembered Saul/Paul a young teacher of the law who could do it much better.

Ten years earlier, Saul met Barnabas when Saul was first saved and came to Jerusalem. But Saul didn't stay in Jerusalem, he headed back to Tarsus to escape the murderous plots of some of his former colleagues. Barnabas remembered the zeal with which

Saul had taught the Old Testament Scriptures from a messianic perspective. In Barnabas's mind, there was no one more needed in Antioch at that time than Saul of Tarsus, so he made the trip to the Asian city of Tarsus to find him. "And when he had found him, he brought him to Antioch" (Acts 11:26).

Together, Barnabas and Saul faithfully ministered to the disciples at Antioch during the next year (A.D. 43). A great many people were taught the Scripture. Not only did the disciples of Antioch acquire an understanding of the content of the Old Testament Scriptures, they began to apply the eternal principles of the Scriptures to their daily lifestyle. This resulted in their earning a Christian reputation in their community, "And the disciples were first called Christians in Antioch" (Acts 11:26).

Barnabas had met Saul in Jerusalem and they apparently became friends. Both of these men had roots outside of Judea. Both knew that much of the world of that time had not heard about Jesus and would be as responsive to the gospel as the Gentiles had been in Antioch. As Barnabas and Saul thought about this matter together, they felt God leading them into a unique ministry of taking the gospel to other cities where there was no Christian church.

As a number of the church leaders in Antioch were fasting together, the Holy Spirit told them, "Now separate to Me Barnabas and Saul for the work to which I have called them" (Acts 13:2). After a further period of fasting, the church laid hands on these two men to identify them as their missionary representatives and sent them on the first missionary journey.

Barnabas and Saul began their missionary journey by heading for the port city of Seleucia and getting on a boat to Cyprus. Barnabas had sold his real estate holdings on the island a number of years before, but likely he still had some contact with old friends and associates on the island. He may have planned to contact them as he and Saul began to evangelize the island. Also, a number of those who had begun the church in Antioch had roots on the Mediterranean island and may have notified their friends and relatives to prepare for the coming of these apostles.

In that first missionary trip, a shift in leadership occurred. It began "Barnabas and Saul" (Acts 13:2). But after a confrontation with a sorcerer, Bar-Jesus, God's power flowed through Saul, and the sorcerer was struck blind. Also at that time Saul's name was changed. "Then Saul, who also is called Paul" (Acts 13:9). Barnabas seemed to take the demotion without incident (we don't know his inner reaction).

But when Paul and Barnabas planned to take a second trip, a disagreement broke out. "Barnabas agreed and wanted to take along John Mark. But Paul disagreed strongly, since John Mark had deserted them in Pamphylia and had not continued with them in their work. Their disagreement was so sharp that they separated. Barnabas took John Mark with him and sailed for Cyprus" (Acts 15:37-39, NLT). Was this evidence that Barnabas was imperfect or was both Paul and Barnabas imperfect? Learn a lesson about disagreement among believers: two can disagree, "Their disagreement was so sharp" (Acts 15:39), yet God can use both you and the one disagreeing with you. Does that mean you are both imperfect? Probably!

LESSONS TO TAKE AWAY

Even those who are conscientious and attempt to follow the Lord in every way are in reality imperfect. When Paul and Barnabas disagreed—sharply—this was evidence of imperfection, in probably both men. What does that say to you? First, you are never perfect. We are all imperfect when measured by God's standards. Second, be careful when arguing with another believer about the "perfect" thing to do. Be willing to back off and look at the situation through someone else's eyes. When you are discussing with another believer about the perfect thing to do, remember your arguing reveals your imperfection. Also, your arguing means you are wrong.

Another practical suggestion! The Rich Young Ruler/Barnabas had a history of claiming perfection. Also, Saul/Paul had the same problem with his history. Remember the advice of Paul, "Don't think you are better than you really are" (Romans 12:3, NLT). There is more advice, "If you think you are too important...you are only fooling yourself" (Galatians 6:3, NLT).

Chapter 10

SAUL/PAUL

The Consummate Legalist
Finally Gains Perfection

THE most imperfect of all persons is the man who probably thinks he is the most perfect of all persons. Not only did this person write a description of his perfection, and all the things he did to gain perfection, he faultlessly carried out his perfection in attitude and actions. But more than that, this man who thought he was perfect hated anyone who denied his standards or broke his standards. As a Jew, he hated all Gentiles and had nothing to do with Gentiles who did not live by his law. But when Jews became Christians and no longer recognized the Old Testament laws and even violated that law, he hated them, attacked them, and did as much as he could to destroy them and kill as many as possible.

It was not that they no longer lived by his law, but their freedom to ignore his standard of law not only irritated him, it rebuked his perfectionism and condemned all that he was. He was driven by his legalistic perfection to hatred...despisal...and retaliation.

Saul, the Jewish rabbi who was perfect in his own eyes, ultimately met Jesus Christ, the only perfect One to ever live on this earth (2 Corinthians 5:21; Hebrews 4:15; 1 Peter 2:21; 1 John 3:5).

When Saul met Jesus, his name was changed to Paul, the apostle who said:

"Even though I used to blaspheme the name of Christ. In my insolence, I persecuted his people. But God had mercy on me because I did it in ignorance and unbelief. Oh, how generous and gracious our Lord was! He filled me with the faith and love that come from Christ Jesus. This is a trustworthy saying, and everyone should accept it: 'Christ Jesus came into the world to save sinners'—and I am the worst of them all." (1 Timothy 1:13-15, NLT).

SAUL'S LAW KEEPING WAS IMPERFECT

Every Old Testament Jew including Saul looked forward to the coming of Messiah who would bring peace and righteousness to the world. But they also looked for the Messiah who would take away all their sins. Think of all the animals slain for the sins of every Jew living in the world. Saul, like every other Jew, should had been looking for the coming of Messiah. But when Messiah came, Saul missed it.

There is one occasion where Bible scholars think that the unsaved Saul may have met Jesus Christ; of His earthly ministry he writes, "Though we have known Christ after the flesh" (2 Corinthians 5:16, KJV). In what sense did Saul know Christ? As a young rabbi in Jerusalem, did he go to hear one of the sermons of Jesus Christ, or was there an occasion where he might have viewed Jesus in the temple, or perhaps he heard about some of the miracles Jesus was doing, or perhaps he was present when Jesus spoke or performed a miracle? That verse continues, "How differently we know him now!"

How "perfect" was the unsaved Saul, at least in his own expectations? "I was circumcised when I was eight days old. I am a pure-blooded citizen of Israel and a member of the tribe of Benjamin—a real Hebrew if there ever was one! I was a member of the Pharisees, who demand the strictest obedience to the Jewish law. I was so zealous that I harshly persecuted the church. And as for righteousness, I obeyed the law without fault" (Philippians 3:5-6, NLT).

And what do we know about Saul? He was a law keeper, but a flawed law keeper. He hated Christ and persecuted Christians. "And Saul was consenting unto his death (Stephen)....there was a great persecution against the church...from house to house... throwing them in prison" (Acts 8:3, KJV). Those were his retaliatory actions. Why did he do that? Saul was filled with inner rage against Christianity. Did they have something he was missing? Did they

have something he did not have? "Saul was uttering threats with every breath and was eager to kill the Lord's followers" (Acts 9:1, NLT).

So what does this tell us, the world's most perfect law keeper, was imperfect. Like any of us who are saved, or those who are lost, we are all imperfect people no matter how hard we try, no matter what good deeds we do, no matter how often we convince ourselves that we are perfect; we are imperfect, and we are lost.

We know that Paul was converted, which involves an entire commitment of one's intellect, emotions, and will to Jesus Christ. You must know (intellect) you are lost and far from God and need salvation from hell. You must feel (emotions) remorse for your sins and at the same time knowing you will go to hell and judgment. But the will (power of choice) is involved. You must decide to follow Jesus Christ, acknowledging that He died for your sins, but also acknowledging His resurrection gives you a new life—eternal life. With this decision you accept Jesus Christ into your life as both Savior from sin and Lord to control your life.

SAUL (MEANS TO ASK) BECOMES PAUL (MEANS SMALL ONE OR HUMBLE)

Saul had been present when Stephen was stoned, but not just as an innocent bystander, "Those who stoned him, laid down their clothes at a young man's feet, whose name was Saul" (Acts 7:58, KJV). By this, "Saul was consenting unto his death" (Acts 8:1).

Most Bible teachers believe that Stephen's death made a profound impact on young Saul and prompted him to give Christianity a deeper examination.

Saul had received official letters from the high priest to go to Damascus to arrest any Jews who were following Jesus Christ. Perhaps as Saul passed through the northern parts of the Holy Land he passed places where Jesus had preached to the multitudes or performed miracles. Do you think any memory of these events weighed upon his mind?

But not until Saul was getting close to the walls of Damascus did anything happen. God let him get almost to his destination before Divine intervention.

"Suddenly a light shown around him from heaven" (Acts 9:3). As this blinding light appeared, Saul fell to the ground probably trying to look away or shield his eyes. Behind this bright light a thunderous voice was heard. Later the Bible describes those with him only heard a noise, yet Saul understood the voice clearly. It was a statement directed at him.

"Saul, Saul, why are you persecuting Me?" (Acts 9:4).

Later Saul/Paul would write letters to remind Christians that they were the "body of Christ." Although Saul did not realize it at the time, when he persecuted Christians, he was actually persecuting Jesus Christ. Only later would Paul and other Christians realize how inclusive this statement might be because of the words of the Lord Jesus, "You in me and I in you" (John 14:20, NLT).

"Who are you, Lord?" (Acts 9:5), Paul responded.

Notice Saul called the voice *Lord*. You think he understood this was the Lord Jesus Christ? Do you think this was simply a Jewish rabbi calling out to God in heaven using the title *Lord*?

There could be no doubt in the answer, the voice replied, "I am Jesus, whom you are persecuting" (Acts 9:5).

As the light suddenly appeared and blinded Saul, many thoughts must have quicly crossed his mind. Was this the Elohim God of the Old Testament speaking to him? Was he wrong about his Old Testament predictions? Was this voice Jesus? Inside Saul was filled with conflicting emotions. Part of him was

shocked into an astonishing insight about the Jews he was persecuting and this Jesus they followed. Had he made a vast miscalculation. But probably another part of Saul was terrified and caused him to realize the God of heaven was speaking to him with a new truth and a new revelation. Did the memory of Stephen's death flash through his mind?

Remember, Saul had been motivated by his zeal for God to go to Damascus. Now, he was almost to Damascus—within sight of the walls—and here he faced the dilemma of his life.

However, even in this moment of confusion, Saul was eager to please the God of the Old Testament he served. He cried out, "Lord, what would you have me to do?"

As quickly as the light appeared over the group and blinded Saul, it faded away. The men with Saul were confused. They heard the noise of the voice, but they did not understand what it was saying. As Saul rose from the ground and tried to open his eyes, he discovered he was blind.

His traveling companions had to lead him by the hand into the city of Damascus. They found a room inside the gate of Damascus on the right-hand side of the street called Straight.

For the next three days Paul could not see and he did not eat...he fasted. Was he physically unable to eat, or did he choose to fast seeking the mind of and presence of God? Paul spent the next three days praying. The voice had told him he would learn more when he arrived in Damascus. Now he was there.

God had revealed Himself to Paul, telling him that a man named Ananias was coming to lay hands on him so he could see again (Acts 9:12). It is interesting that God told Paul that Ananias was coming, but at the same time God was speaking to Ananias telling him to go and lay hands on Paul so he could receive his sight.

"So Ananias went and found Saul. He laid his hands on him and said, 'Brother Saul, the Lord Jesus, who appeared to you on the road has sent me so that you might receive your sight and be filled with the Holy Spirit.' Instantly, something like scales feel from Saul's eyes, and he regained his sight. Then he got up and was baptized. Afterwords he ate some food and regained his strength" (Acts 9:17-18, NLT).

The church in Jerusalem had been warned about Saul's coming and the persecution he would bring. When one of the disciples named Ananias received a vision in which the Lord told him to go to the house of Judas on Straight Street to find Saul of Tarsus, he was sure there was some mistake. "But Lord," exclaimed Ananias, 'I've heard many people talk about the terrible things this man has done to the believers in Jerusalem! And he is authorized by the leading priests to arrest everyone who calls upon your name" (Acts 9:13-14, NLT).

Paul's decision to embrace Jesus as Messiah meant something new to him. Now he was in danger. Those who had come to Damascus with him to persecute the followers of Jesus were now his enemy. Saul left his temporary residence of the house of Judas and, "Saul stayed with the believers in Damascus for a few days" (Acts 9:19, NLT).

Some think at this time, Paul went into Arabia (the desert) for three years to study and to receive revelations (Ephesians 3). Others think he went to Arabia (the desert) for 40 days or even 3 days. It's not clear how long Paul spent in the desert, but he returned to the city of Damascus and ministered there (Acts 9:19-22). Then after three years he went to Jerusalem (Acts 9:24-26; Galatians 1:17-18).

During this time, Paul was taught by God. "I did not...consult with any human...nor apostles...went away into Arabia (desert) .... Three years...went to Jerusalem...saw only Peter...only other was James the Lord's brother" (Galatians 1:16-18, NLT).

What was the revelation that God gave to Paul? "God Himself revealed His mysterious plan to me... both Jew and Gentle share equally...both belong to Christ Jesus" (see Ephesians 3:3-6).

LEARNING FROM PAUL

Some people think that repentance from sins involves getting rid of transgressions and disobedience so you can get close to God. They think you need to give up cussing, give up strong drink, adultery, and lying.

The Greek word for repentance—*metanoya* means—"to change one's mind." As you change your mind about Jesus Christ, you change your feelings and your desires, and ultimately your lifestyle.

And what is the first lesson to learn? You learn that you have an old nature "your old sinful nature makes you want to sin" (Ephesians 4:23, ELT). Even though Saul was a legalist, he still had an old sinful nature. All have that old nature until Christ gives them a new nature.

The next thing to learn is that the old nature enslaves your life. Paul said, "I want to do what is good, but I don't. I don't want to do what is wrong, but I do it anyway" (Romans 7:19, NLT). There is a battle that goes on inside the heart of the unsaved; it is between that which is good and evil. Even though a person is born again, the old nature will always pull him/her towards evil and that which is wrong.

The third lesson to learn is that our new nature gives us new power and new desires and a new purpose in life. Paul tells us, "Put on your new nature" (Ephesians 4:24, NLT). This new nature is the Person of Jesus Christ who comes to dwell in our hearts, He influences every part of our inner person, our thinking, our desires, our decisions, as well as our self-perception and self-direction.

How does this happen? When Christ was crucified, we died with Him. When He was raised to new life, we raised with Him. Paul explains this truth to us in the picture of baptism, "For we died and were buried with Christ...And just as Christ was raised from the dead by the glorious power of the Father, now we also may live new lives. Since we have been united with him in his death, we will also be raised to life as he was" (Romans 6:4-5, NLT).

Paul explains it at another place, "My old self has been crucified with Christ...Christ lives in me" (Galatians 2:20, NLT).

I was saved on July 25, 1950 at a revival in Bonnabella, Georgia. I had just graduated from high school. Immediately, I gave up my plans to go to Georgia Tech and/or Armstrong State University in Savannah, Georgia. I surrendered to ministry and went to Columbia Bible College. While there, I was a typical freshmen. I was involved in Halloween pranks, and according to the testimony of my roommate, on several occasions I irritated them with practical jokes and immature actions.

However, the following Easter Sunday morning, I waited for my ride to my Christian service assignment, which was approximately 30 minutes late due to time change Sunday. I stood in the warm spring sunlight to meditate on Galatians 2:20, focusing on two truths. First, I focused on Christ in me. Second was an even more weightier obligation since I was crucified with Christ, I had to nail my sinful desires along with my pranks and everything else that irritated my roommate to the cross to die with Jesus. I surrendered, making Jesus Christ the Lord of my life. I promised to let Him rule all my decisions. That was a life-changing moment.

Once you make that decision, you have a new passion in life. Paul expressed it, "For to me, living means living for Christ" (Philippians 1:21, NLT). Therefore, everything in life is measured by the phrase "Living for Jesus." Since He lives in you, you must let Him live through you.

But I also found a new power in Jesus, "I can do everything through Christ who gives me strength" (Philippians 4:13, NLT). I experience power in my life that Paul experienced in his life, and that power is Jesus Christ living through me.

LESSONS TO TAKE AWAY

Remember Paul thought he was perfect and in every way he tried to be as perfect as possible. Yet he was unusable because he was unsaved. There are some Christians who are useable because they do everything in their own strength and in their own way for their own purpose. But when they realize they are unusable, then they can take the first step to usability.

Only as they see their imperfections as Jesus sees them can they begin to accept Him and His presence into their life and let His power work through them to accomplish His will. What happens to them can happen to you. That means you can be used by Him, even if you are imperfect.

All of this involves faith; you must believe what God has said in His Word, which is believing the promises that Jesus has made to you. But more than belief, you must apply them to your life and act upon them. Remember you spell "faith" as F-A-I-T-H. That means, *forsaking all I take Him.*

After all, doesn't faith make us acceptable to God so that He can use us as we are? When we realize we are unusable, and we claim His indwelling presence and power, then we can be used of Him to accomplish His purpose for His glory.

The more we see our imperfections through the eyes of Jesus, the more we will trust in His forgiveness to accept us, and His power to use us. It is then that God can do through us what He plans for us.

Aren't you glad you are imperfect? We are all sinners and we are all imperfect, so recognize your imperfections and let it be the starting place for God's usefulness. When you begin with sin—putting it under the blood—then you are in a place where God can use you.

What is the main lesson you can learn from Paul? The consummate legalist finally gained perfection in Jesus Christ and was used of Him.

PART TWO

LEARNING FROM
GOD'S IMPERFECT PEOPLE

LESSONS

WHY GOD USES IMPERFECTIONS

A. IMPERFECT PEOPLE?

1. <u>Positive</u>: we learn victory is possible when God gives weak people strength to succeed.

2. <u>Negative</u>: we learn what not to do.

TEN IMPERFECT PEOPLE

- Jacob: A liar and trickster changed by a <u>**dream**</u>

- Noah: After walking with God got <u>**drunk**</u>

- Peter: A granite rock who <u>**cracked**</u>

- Gideon: God pushed him to <u>**victory**</u>

- Thomas: A Jesus follower who <u>**doubted**</u>

- Naomi: A bitter woman constantly desiring better, ended up a <u>**nourisher**</u>

- Samson: Wrongly <u>**trusted**</u> in his own strength

- Solomon: The world's <u>**wisest**</u> made bad choices

- Rich Young Ruler: A wealthy man learned <u>**value**</u>

- Saul/Paul: The consummate legalist finally gains <u>**perfection**</u>

3. We learn we have <u>sinned</u>. "For all have sinned and missed God's presence" (see Romans 3:23).

4. We learn we were <u>blinded</u> by our sin. "Satan, who is the god of this world, has blinded the minds of those who don't believe. They are unable to see the glorious light of the Good News. They don't understand this message about the glory of Christ, who is the exact likeness of God" (2 Corinthians 4:4, NLT).

5. We learn our <u>good habits</u> and deeds are worthless. "All have turned away; all have become useless. No one does good, not a single one" (Romans 3:12, NLT).

6. We are <u>slaves</u> to our old nature and sin. "I want to do what is good, but I don't. I don't want to do what is wrong, but I do it anyway. But if I do what I don't want to do, I am not really the one doing wrong; it is sin living in me that does it" (Romans 7:19-20, NLT).

B. THE BOOK OF JUDGES IS ABOUT WEAK LEADERS, I.E., IMPERFECT PEOPLE

"The Israelites did evil in the Lord's sight and served the images of Baal. They abandoned the Lord, the God of their ancestors, who had brought them out of Egypt. They went after other gods, worshiping the gods of the people around them. And they angered the Lord. They abandoned the Lord to serve Baal and the images of Ashtoreth" (Judges 2:11-13, NLT).

Things they did.

1. No <u>belief</u>. "Forsook the Lord" (2:12).

2. No <u>obedience</u>. "Turned quickly from the way" (2:17).

3. Did the <u>opposite</u>. "Served Baal and Ashtoreths" (2:13).

4. <u>Flaunted evil</u>. "Did evil in the sight of the Lord" (2:11).

C. WHY GOD USES IMPERFECT PEOPLE

1. For **His glory**. "Now all glory to God, who is able to make you strong" (Romans 16:25, NLT).

2. As a testimony to the **unsaved**. "Remember...few of you were wise in the world's eyes, or powerful, or wealthy...instead God chose things the world considers foolish...considered weak ... considered despised...to bring to nothing what the world considers important...so no one can ever boast in the presence of God" (1 Corinthians 1:26-29, NLT).

3. To **demonstrate** the power of God. "The message of the cross...is the very power of God" (1 Corinthians 1:18, NLT).

WHY GOD USES IMPERFECT PEOPLE

- So people will see God, **not man**

- So people will worship God **unreservedly**

- So people will be motivated to **service**

- So Christ's body will **work** together

- Because God **strategy** uses imperfect people

D. WHAT IS THE PRINCIPLE?

1. **Not I but Christ**. Let Christ shine above your weaknesses. "I am crucified with Christ, nevertheless I live, yet not I, but Christ who dwells in me and the life which I live in the flesh I live by the faith of the son of God" (see Galatians 2:20).

2. So God's work is not done in a **worldly way**. "You don't see among yourselves many of the wise ... many of the ruling class...many of the **nobles**...who are called" (1 Corinthians 1:26, Phillips).

3. For God to **work through us**. "My strength (Christ) is made perfect in weakness" (2 Corinthians 12:9).

4. To manifest **God's power**. "My (Christ) power shows up best through weak people" (2 Corinthians 12:9, LB).

5. God calls a man/woman then does His work through them. "The Lord raised up a deliverer" (Judges 3:9).

6. To **glorify God**. "God has chosen the weak things...that no flesh should glory in His presence" (1 Corinthians 1:27-29).

7. But don't stay "imperfect."

    a. Get a **vision** of what you can do.

    b. Find **God's plan** for your life (Jeremiah 29:11).

    c. Don't focus your life on your **weaknesses**.

    d. Work from your **strength**, that will lift your weaknesses. "I can do all things through Christ who strengthen me" (Philippians 4:13).

WHY GOD USES IMPERFECTIONS

A. IMPERFECT PEOPLE?

1. _____ : we learn victory is possible when God gives weak people strength to succeed.

2. _____ : we learn what not to do.

TEN IMPERFECT PEOPLE

- Jacob: A liar and trickster changed by a _____

- Noah: After walking with God got _____

- Peter: A granite rock who cracked

- Gideon: God pushed him to _____

- Thomas: A Jesus follower who _____

- Naomi: A bitter woman constantly desiring better, ended up a _____

- Samson: Wrongly _____ in his own strength

- Solomon: The world's _____ made bad choices

- Rich Young Ruler: A wealthy man learned _____

- Saul/Paul: The consummate legalist finally gains _____

3. We learn we have sinned. "For all have sinned and missed God's presence" (Romans 3:23, ELT).

4. We learn we were _____ by our sin. "Satan, who is the god of this world, has blinded the minds of those who don't believe. They are unable to see the glorious light of the Good News. They don't understand this message about the glory of Christ, who is the exact likeness of God" (2 Corinthians 4:4, NLT).

5. We learn our _____ and deeds are worthless. "All have turned away; all have become useless. No one does good, not a single one" (Romans 3:12, NLT).

6. We are _____ to our old nature and sin. "I want to do what is good, but I don't. I don't want to do what is wrong, but I do it anyway. But if I do what I don't want to do, I am not really the one doing wrong; it is sin living in me that does it" (Romans 7:19-20, NLT).

B. THE BOOK OF JUDGES IS ABOUT WEAK LEADERS, I.E., IMPERFECT PEOPLE

"The Israelites did evil in the Lord's sight and served the images of Baal. They abandoned the Lord, the God of their ancestors, who had brought them out of Egypt. They went after other gods, worshiping the gods of the people around them. And they angered the Lord. They abandoned the Lord to serve Baal and the images of Ashtoreth" (Judges 2:11-13, NLT).

Things they did.

1. No _____ . "Forsook the Lord" (2:12).

2. No _____ . "Turned quickly from the way" (2:17).

3. Did the _____ . "Served Baal and Ashtoreths" (2:13).

4. _____ . "Did evil in the sight of the Lord" (2:11).

C. WHY GOD USES IMPERFECT PEOPLE

1. For _____ . "Now all glory to God, who is able to make you strong" (Romans 16:25, NLT).

2. As a testimony to the _____ . "Remember...few of you were wise in the world's eyes, or powerful, or wealthy...instead God chose things the world considers foolish...considered weak ... considered despised...to bring to nothing what the world considers important...so no one can ever boast in the presence of God" (1 Corinthians 1:26-29, NLT).

3. To _____ the power of God. "The message of the cross...is the very power of God" (1 Corinthians 1:18, NLT).

WHY GOD USES IMPERFECT PEOPLE

*   So people will see God, _____
*   So people will worship God _____
*   So people will be motivated to _____
*   So Christ's body will _____ together
*   Because God _____ uses imperfect people

D. WHAT IS THE PRINCIPLE?

1. _____ . Let Christ shine above your weaknesses. "I am crucified with Christ, nevertheless I live, yet not I, but Christ who dwells in me and the life which I live in the flesh I live by the faith of the son of God" (see Galatians 2:20).

2. So God's work is not done in a _____ . "You don't see among yourselves many of the wise ... many of the ruling class...many of the _____ ...who are called" (1 Corinthians 1:26, Phillips).

3. For God to _____ . "My strength (Christ) is made perfect in weakness" (2 Corinthians 12:9).

4. To manifest _____ . "My (Christ) power shows up best through weak people" (2 Corinthians 12:9, LB).

5. God calls a man/woman then does His work through them. "The Lord raised up a deliverer" (Judges 3:9).

6. To _____ . "God has chosen the weak things...that no flesh should glory in His presence" (1 Corinthians 1:27-29).

7. But don't stay "imperfect."

    a. Get a _____ of what you can do.

    b. Find _____ for your life (Jeremiah 29:11).

    c. Don't focus your life on your _____ .

    d. Work from your _____ , that will lift your weaknesses. "I can do all things through Christ who strengthen me" (Philippians 4:13).

Lesson 1:

ANSWER KEY

JACOB
A Liar And Trickster Changed By A Dream

A. JACOB WAS PERFECTLY IMPERFECT

1. He enticed his brother Esau to sell his family birthright (Genesis 25: 26-34).

2. He deceived his father and lied to get the family's inheritance (Genesis 27:1-33).

3. Jacob had to run away from home. "Esau hated Jacob...'I will kill my brother'" (Genesis 27:41).

4. A dream from God changed his focus. "He dreamed...a ladder...the Lord stood above it...the land whereupon thou liest, to thee will I give it, and to thy seed" (Genesis 28:12-14, KJV).

   a. The land now has Jacob's new name – **Israel**.

   b. The people have Jacob's new name – **the children of Israel**.

5. Twenty years later, Jacob wrestles all night with a Christophany (the person of God). "When the man saw that he would not win the match, he touched Jacob's hip, and wrenched it out of its socket...'I will not let you go unless you bless me'" (Genesis 32;25-26, NLT).

6. Name changed from Jacob the **deceiver**, to Israel **prince with God**. "Thy name shall be called no more Jacob, but Israel: for as a prince thou hast power with God and with men, and hast prevailed" (Genesis 32:28, KJV).

7. Even through a deceiver and imperfect, Jacob's **deep heart decision** was for God's blessing.

8. What can we learn? Deep passionate, sacrificial faith **pleases God** (Hebrews 11:6).

B. WHY WAS JACOB IMPERFECT?

1. His mother Rebekah was **as deceptive** as Jacob (Genesis 27:5-10).

2. His father was old and invalid (27:1), did not influence Jacob.

3. He had no **role models** to do right.

C. TO CHALLENGE AND CHANGE IMPERFECT PEOPLE

1. Jacob defined by a **dream** of a ladder and God at the top (Genesis 27:12-22).

   a. Jacob left home in **obedience**. "Jacob obeyed his parents" (see 28:7).

   b. Jacob was reminded by God to make a mighty nation of his children (28:2-4).

   c. Jacob **encountered** God, "I am the LORD, God of your grandfather Abraham ... your father Isaac" (28:13, NLT).

   d. Jacob was promised the **land**. "The ground you are lying on ... I am giving it to you" (28:13, NLT).

   e. Jacob was promised God's **presence**. "I am with you and will protect you" (see 28:15).

2. Jacob encountered God's presence twenty years later.

   a. Threat from his **father-in-law**. "Laban caught ... Laban demanded...Laban challenged, why did you deceive me" (see 31:25-27).

   b. Threat from **brother**. "Esau came, and with him four hundred men" (33:1, KJV).

   c. Threat from an **intruder**. "Left Jacob all alone, and man came and wrestled with him until the dawn" (32:24, NLT). A Christophany an appearance of God. "Jacob named the place Penial (which means 'face of God'), for he said, 'I have seen God face to face...'" (32:30, NLT).

3. Every imperfect believer needs:

   a. A dream: (1) to be reminded **who you are**, (2) to keep your focus of **God's future**, (3) to **motive you and empower** you.

   b. An encounter with God must demonstrate: (1) to show God your **determination** to serve Him, (2) to let **God** "touch" you, (3) to see **God's face**.

JACOB

A Liar And Trickster Changed By A Dream

A. JACOB WAS PERFECTLY IMPERFECT

1. He enticed his brother Esau to sell his family birthright (Genesis 25: 26-34).

2. He deceived his father and lied to get the family's inheritance (Genesis 27:1-33).

3. Jacob had to run away from home. "Esau hated Jacob...'I will kill my brother'" (Genesis 27:41).

4. A dream from God changed his focus. "He dreamed...a ladder...the Lord stood above it...the land whereupon thou liest, to thee will I give it, and to thy seed" (Genesis 28:12-14, KJV).

   a. The land now has Jacob's new name – _____ .

   b. The people have Jacob's new name – _____ .

5. Twenty years later, Jacob wrestles all night with a Christophany (the person of God). "When the man saw that he would not win the match, he touched Jacob's hip, and wrenched it out of its socket...'I will not let you go unless you bless me'" (Genesis 32;25-26, NLT).

6. Name changed from Jacob the _____ , to Israel _____ . "Thy name shall be called no more Jacob, but Israel: for as a prince thou hast power with God and with men, and hast prevailed" (Genesis 32:28, KJV).

7. Even through a deceiver and imperfect, Jacob's _____ was for God's blessing.

8. What can we learn? Deep passionate, sacrificial faith _____ (Hebrews 11:6).

B. WHY WAS JACOB IMPERFECT?

1. His mother Rebekah was _____ as Jacob (Genesis 27:5-10).

2. His father was old and invalid (27:1), did not influence Jacob.

3. He had no _____ to do right.

C. TO CHALLENGE AND CHANGE IMPERFECT PEOPLE

1. Jacob defined by a _____ of a ladder and God at the top (Genesis 27:12-22).

   a. Jacob left home in _____ . "Jacob obeyed his parents" (see 28:7).

   b. Jacob was reminded by God to make a mighty nation of his children (28:2-4).

   c. Jacob _____ God, "I am the LORD, God of your grandfather Abraham ... your father Isaac" (28:13, NLT).

   d. Jacob was promised the _____ . "The ground you are lying on ... I am giving it to you" (28:13, NLT).

   e. Jacob was promised God's _____ . "I am with you and will protect you" (see 28:15).

2. Jacob encountered God's presence twenty years later.

   a. Threat from his _____ . "Laban caught ... Laban demanded...Laban challenged, why did you deceive me" (see 31:25-27).

   b. Threat from _____ . "Esau came, and with him four hundred men" (33:1, KJV).

   c. Threat from an _____ . Left Jacob all alone, and man came and wrestled with him until the dawn" (32:24, NLT). A Christophany an appearance of God. "Jacob named the place Penial (which means 'face of God'), for he said, 'I have seen God face to face...'" (32:30, NLT).

3. Every imperfect believer needs:

   a. A dream: (1) to be reminded _____ , (2) to keep your focus of _____ , (3) to _____ you.

   b. An encounter with God must demonstrate: (1) to show God your _____ to serve Him, (2) to let _____ "touch" you, (3) to see _____ .

NOAH
After Walking With God, He Got Drunk

A. WHAT NOAH DID FOR GOD

1. **Godly**. What is known about Noah? "Noah was a just man and perfect   ...and Noah walked with God" (see Genesis 6:9).

2. **Warned of judgment**. Why did Noah build an ark? "By faith Noah being divinely warned of things not yet seen moved with godly fear, prepared an ark...by which he condemned the world" (Hebrews 11:7).

3. **Carpenter**. What was Noah's occupation? "God said to Noah...make yourself an ark of gopherwood" (Genesis 6:14).

4. **Preacher**. How did Noah warn the world? "Noah...a preacher of righteousness" (2 Peter 2:5).

5. **Drinking**. What sins did Jesus mention that Noah preached against?" As the days of Noah were, so also will be the coming of the Son of Man...drinking...until the day Noah entered the ark" (Matthew 24:37-38).

6. **Satan worship**. What were other sins the people committed? (Genesis 6:1-13).

7. **God called**. When did Noah enter the ark? "The Lord said to Noah, 'Come thou and all thy house into the ark'" (Genesis 7:1, KJV). He was 600 years old (Genesis 8:13).

B. WHAT NOAH DID WRONG

"And Noah began to be a farmer, and he planted a vineyard. Then he drank of the wine and was drunk, and became uncovered in his tent. And Ham, the father of Canaan, saw the nakedness of his father, and told his two brothers outside. But Shem and Japheth took a garment, laid it on both their shoulders, and went backward and covered the nakedness of their father. Their faces were turned away, and they did not see their father's nakedness. So Noah awoke from his wine, and knew what his younger son had done to him. Then he said: 'Cursed be Canaan; a servant of servants He shall be to his brethren'" (Genesis 9:20-25).

1. **A farmer**. What was Noah's new occupation after the flood? "Noah began to be a husbandman, and he planted a vineyard" (9:20, KJV).

2. What was Noah's threefold sin? "He (Noah) drank of the wine, and was drunken, and he was uncovered within the tent" (Genesis 9:21, KJV).

    a. **Drunken**. He preached against it.

    b. **Exposure**. He uncovered himself, i.e., *gulah* (reflective)

    c. **Lack of role model**.

3. How did Noah know? "Noah awoke from his wine, and knew what his younger son had done to him" (9:24).

    a. Special **revelation**.

    b. **Inquiry**. He asked or was told.

    c. **Memory**. A drunk man remembers some things.

C. WHAT WAS THE SIN OF HAM AND CANAAN?

Grandfather—Noah—sinned

Father—Ham—gossiped

Grandson—Canaan—laughed

1. **Seeing only**. "Ham, the father of Canaan saw the nakedness of his father, and told his two brethren" (Genesis 9:22, KJV). What went with seeing?

   a. **Lust**.

   b. Mockery.

   c. **Rejection** of father's authority to His God. (Morris)

   d. Not covering, i.e., showing disrespect.

2. **Not seeing**. "Shem and Japheth took a garment, and laid it upon their shoulders, and went backward, and covered the nakedness of their father;...and saw not their father's nakedness" (Genesis 9:23, KJV).

3. Why curse Canaan?

   a. **Youngest**. Ham was the youngest son of Noah, and Canaan youngest son of Ham (Genesis 10:6).

   b. **Divine curse**. This was not an "angry" grandfather. Since only God could know the future, Noah spoke by God's revelation. God cursed Canaan for what he did, and what he was to become.

   c. Noah recognized a rebellious attitude and perverse lust. Noah/God saw a weakness in Canaan and knew it would be perpetuated.

   d. **Third generation** always suffers the most, "cursed be Canaan; a servant of servants, shall he be unto his brethren" (Genesis 9:25, KJV).

4. When was the curse carried out?

   a. The Canaanites become a **lustful people**. God describes them "uncovered the nakedness" (Leviticus 18:3 ff).

   b. The curse was carried out when Joshua and Israel **conquered** the Canaanites (Joshua 11-12).

D. WHAT LESSONS CAN BE LEARNED ABOUT SINNING GRANDPARENTS

1. You never get **too old to quit sinning**.

2. You can fall at your greatest strength. "Let him that thinketh he standeth take heed lest he fall" (1 Corinthians 10:12).

3. Your fall can hurt **your family**. "Cursed be Canaan."

4. Your fall can come after God has greatly used you. Noah, Elijah, Peter, Paul, Uriah, David.

5. Just because you have done a lot for God, doesn't mean He will **overlook your sin in old age**.

6. The careless root of sin in a grandfather or father (lust or rebellion) can have disastrous results in grandchildren.

7. Drunkenness is not a **private sin**, nor is it something God overlooks.

8. The body is the temple of the Holy Spirit, and the child of God should be modest.

    a. Applies to all ages.

    b. Applies to **sexual exposure**.

    c. Applies to **sexual viewing, i.e., lust**.

E. WHAT YOU NEED TO KNOW

1. God **provides victory**. "No temptation has overtaken you except such as is common to man; but God is faithful, who will not allow you to be tempted beyond what you are able, but with the temptation will also make the way of escape, that you may be able to bear it" (1 Corinthians 10:13).

2. God **lives in your body**. "He who commits sexual immorality, sins against his own body. Do you not know that your body is the temple of the Holy Spirit, who is in you...you are not your own" (1 Corinthians 6:18-19).

3. Old age sin **will disqualify you**. "But I discipline my body and bring it into subjection, lest, when I have preached to others, I myself should become disqualified" (1 Corinthians 9:27).

Lesson 2:

QUESTIONS

NOAH

After Walking With God, He Got Drunk

A. WHAT NOAH DID FOR GOD

1. _____ . What is known about Noah? "Noah was a just man and perfect ...and Noah walked with God" (see Genesis 6:9).

2. _____ . Why did Noah build an ark? "By faith Noah being divinely warned of things not yet seen moved with godly fear, prepared an ark...by which he condemned the world" (Hebrews 11:7).

3. _____ . What was Noah's occupation? "God said to Noah...make yourself an ark of gopherwood" (Genesis 6:14).

4. _____ . How did Noah warn the world? "Noah...a preacher of righteousness" (2 Peter 2:5).

5. _____ . What sins did Jesus mention that Noah preached against?" As the days of Noah were, so also will be the coming of the Son of Man...drinking...until the day Noah entered the ark" (Matthew 24:37-38).

6. _____ . What were other sins the people committed? (Genesis 6:1-13).

7. _____ . When did Noah enter the ark? "The Lord said to Noah, 'Come thou and all thy house into the ark'" (Genesis 7:1). He was 600 years old (Genesis 8:13, KJV).

B. WHAT NOAH DID WRONG

"And Noah began to be a farmer, and he planted a vineyard. Then he drank of the wine and was drunk, and became uncovered in his tent. And Ham, the father of Canaan, saw the nakedness of his father, and told his two brothers outside. But Shem and Japheth took a garment, laid it on both their shoulders, and went backward and covered the nakedness of their father. Their faces were turned away, and they did not see their father's nakedness. So Noah awoke from his wine, and knew what his younger son had done to him. Then he said: 'Cursed be Canaan; a servant of servants He shall be to his brethren'" (Genesis 9:20-25).

1. _____ . What was Noah's new occupation after the flood? "Noah began to be a husbandman, and planted a vineyard" (9:20).

2. What was Noah's threefold sin? "He (Noah) drank of the wine, and was drunken, and he was uncovered within the tent" (Genesis 9:21, KJV).

    a. _____ . He preached against it.

    b. _____ . He uncovered himself, i.e., *gulah* (reflective)

    c. _____ .

3. How did Noah know? "Noah awoke from his wine, and knew what his younger son had done to him" (9:24).

    a. Special _____ .

    b. _____ . He asked or was told.

    c. _____ . A drunk man remembers some things.

C. WHAT WAS THE SIN OF HAM AND CANAAN?

Grandfather—Noah—sinned

Father—Ham—gossiped

Grandson—Canaan—laughed

1. _____ . "Ham, the father of Canaan saw the nakedness of his father, and told his two brethren" (Genesis 9:22, KJV). What went with seeing?

    a. _____ .

    b. Mockery.

    c. _____ of father's authority to His God. (Morris)

    d. Not covering, i.e., showing disrespect.

2. _____ . "Shem and Japheth took a garment, and laid it upon their shoulders, and went backward, and covered the nakedness of their father;...and saw not their father's nakedness" (Genesis 9:23, KJV).

3. Why curse Canaan?

    a. _____ . Ham was the youngest son of Noah, and Canaan youngest son of Ham (Genesis 10:6).

    b. _____ . This was not an "angry" grandfather. Since only God could know the future, Noah spoke by God's revelation. God cursed Canaan for what he did, and what he was to become.

    c. Noah recognized a rebellious attitude and perverse lust. Noah/God saw a weakness in Canaan and knew it would be perpetuated.

    d. _____ always suffers the most, "cursed be Canaan; a servant of servants, shall he be unto his brethren" (Genesis 9:25, KJV).

4. When was the curse carried out?

    a. The Canaanites become a _____ . God describes them "uncovered the nakedness" (see Leviticus 18:3 ff).

    b. The curse was carried out when Joshua and Israel _____ the Canaanites (Joshua 11-12).

D. WHAT LESSONS CAN BE LEARNED ABOUT SINNING GRANDPARENTS

1. You never get _____ .

2. You can fall at your greatest strength. "Let him that thinketh he standeth take heed lest he fall" (1 Corinthians 10:12, KJV).

3. Your fall can hurt _____ . "Cursed be Canaan."

4. Your fall can come after God has greatly used you. Noah, Elijah, Peter, Paul, Uriah, David.

5. Just because you have done a lot for God, doesn't mean He will _____ .

6. The careless root of sin in a grandfather or father (lust or rebellion) can have disastrous results in grandchildren.

7. Drunkenness is not a _____ , nor is it something God overlooks.

8. The body is the temple of the Holy Spirit, and the child of God should be modest.

   a. Applies to all ages.

   b. Applies to _____ .

   c. Applies to _____ .

E. WHAT YOU NEED TO KNOW

1. God _____ . "No temptation has overtaken you except such as is common to man; but God is faithful, who will not allow you to be tempted beyond what you are able, but with the temptation will also make the way of escape, that you may be able to bear it" (1 Corinthians 10:13, NKJV).

2. God _____ . "He who commits sexual immorality, sins against his own body. Do you not know that your body is the temple of the Holy Spirit, who is in you...you are not your own" (1 Corinthians 6:18-19).

3. Old age sin _____ . "But I discipline my body and bring it into subjection, lest, when I have preached to others, I myself should become disqualified" (1 Corinthians 9:27).

PETER

A Granite Rock Chipped

A. PETER THE ROCK

"When Jesus came into the region of Caesarea Philippi, He asked His disciples, saying, 'Who do men say that I, the Son of Man, am?' So they said, 'Some say John the Baptist, some Elijah, and others Jeremiah or one of the prophets.' He said to them, 'But who do you say that I am?' Simon Peter answered and said, 'You are the Christ, the Son of the living God.' Jesus answered and said to him, 'Blessed are you, Simon Bar-Jonah, for flesh and blood has not revealed this to you, but My Father who is in heaven. And I also say to you that you are Peter, and on this rock I will build My church, and the gates of Hades shall not prevail against it'" (Matthew 16:13-18).

1. Jesus asked a question about His **humanity**. "Who do men say that I, the son of Man, am?"

2. The disciples answered:

    •   John the Baptist – famous for **preaching**

    •   Elijah – went to Heaven **without dying**

    •   Jeremiah – to come before **Messiah**

    •   One of the prophets – **Moses** (Deuteronomy 18:18)

3. Jesus asked a **personal** question. "But who do you say that I am?" (v. 15).

    a. You must answer **now**.

    b. You will answer **then**. "Every tongue will confess" (see Philippians 2:11).

B. THE "ROCK" CONFESSION BY PETER

1. The **Christ** means Messiah (Anointed), the coming Son of David to conquer Israel's enemies and rule on the throne. "The Son of the living God," Peter confessed **Jesus' Deity**.

2. Peter was called, Simon Bar-Jonah, i.e., "Son of Jonah" Peter's human **heritage** in contrast to Jesus' divine **Sonship**.

3. Jesus comments – humans didn't tell you this, My **Father** told you this (**Revelation**) (Matthew 16:17).

C. WHAT A ROCK PRODUCES

1. You are Peter (n) *Petros* = **little loose stone**. On this rock (f) *Petra* = **ledge rock** which is his confession.

2. "I will build My church" (v. 18).

   a. "I" – Jesus is the **church planter**.

   b. "Will" – Jesus will plant churches in the **future**.

   c. "Build" – Greek **constant** building.

   d. "My" – the church belongs to Jesus, not a **pastor, deacons, or people**.

   e. "Ecclesia" – the church is a group of **out-called one**.

What Is The Church?

Called from the world—**separate**

Called together—**worship and serve**

3. "Gates of Hell" the church is **attacking**, Satan is defending.

4. Why did Jesus use an imperfect Peter called "rock" (v. 18)?

   a. Rock is **Jesus**. He is the foundation of the church (Ephesians 2:20).

   b. Rock is **message**-confession.

   c. Rock is **soul winner**.

D. PETER REBUKED

"From that time Jesus began to show to His disciples that He must go to Jerusalem, and suffer many things from the elders and chief priests and scribes, and be killed, and be raised the third day. Then Peter took Him aside and began to rebuke Him, saying, 'Far be it from You, Lord; this shall not happen to You!' But He turned and said to Peter, 'Get behind Me, Satan! You are an offense to Me, for you are not mindful of the things of God, but the things of men'" (Matthew 16:21-23).

1. Jesus' death and resurrection shouldn't have <u>**surprised**</u> the disciples (v. 21).

2. You can quickly lose your <u>**usefulness**</u> in God's plan (v. 23).

3. You can quickly go from "mindful of the Father's revelations," to "mindful of man's corrupt plans." Revealing Peter's <u>**imperfection**</u>.

E. PETER THE ROCK—CRACKED

1. <u>**Denial**</u>. "One of the servant girls...noticed Peter warming himself by the fire...and said, 'You were one of those with Jesus of Nazareth.' But Peter denied, 'I don't know what you are talking about.'... 'This man is definitely one of them!' But Peter denied ... a little later...a bystander said, 'You must be one of them, because you are a Galilean' ... Peter cursed" (Mark 14:66-71, NLT).

2. Peter denied <u>**three**</u> times. Jesus asked him three times "Do you love (agape) Me?" Peter confessed, "Lord You know I love (phileo) You" (see John 21:15-17).

3. Jesus <u>**re-instituted**</u> His commission, "Then feed My sheep" (see John 21:17).

4. Jesus uses us when we come <u>**honestly**</u> to Him.

5. Mighty warriors for God can have <u>**feet of clay**</u>.

6. Your strength is not in your personality or your powerful will, it is in <u>**Christ**</u>.

7. What is the main lesson to learn from Peter?

Lesson 3:

QUESTIONS

PETER
A Granite Rock Chipped

A. PETER THE ROCK

"When Jesus came into the region of Caesarea Philippi, He asked His disciples, saying, 'Who do men say that I, the Son of Man, am?' So they said, 'Some say John the Baptist, some Elijah, and others Jeremiah or one of the prophets.' He said to them, 'But who do you say that I am?' Simon Peter answered and said, 'You are the Christ, the Son of the living God.' Jesus answered and said to him, 'Blessed are you, Simon Bar-Jonah, for flesh and blood has not revealed this to you, but My Father who is in heaven. And I also say to you that you are Peter, and on this rock I will build My church, and the gates of Hades shall not prevail against it'" (Matthew 16:13-18).

1. Jesus asked a question about His _____ . "Who do men say that I, the son of Man, am?"

2. The disciples answered:

    • John the Baptist – famous for _____

    • Elijah – went to Heaven _____

    • Jeremiah – to come before _____

    • One of the prophets – _____ (Deuteronomy 18:18)

3. Jesus asked a _____ question. "But who do you say that I am?" (v. 15).

    a. You must answer _____ .

    b. You will answer _____ . "Every tongue will confess" (see Philippians 2:11).

B. THE "ROCK" CONFESSION BY PETER

1. The _____ means Messiah (Anointed), the coming Son of David to conquer Israel's enemies and rule on the throne. "The Son of the living God," Peter confessed _____ .

2. Peter was called, Simon Bar-Jonah, i.e., "Son of Jonah" Peter's human _____ in contrast to Jesus' divine _____ .

3. Jesus comments – humans didn't tell you this, My _____ told you this (_____) (Matthew 16:17).

C. WHAT A ROCK PRODUCES

1. You are Peter (n) *Petros* = _____ .
   On this rock (f) *Petra* = _____ which is his confession.

2. "I will build My church" (v. 18).

   a. "I" – Jesus is the _____ .

   b. "Will" – Jesus will plant churches in the _____ .

   c. "Build" – Greek _____ building.

   d. "My" – the church belongs to Jesus, not a _____ .

   e. "Ecclesia" – the church is a group of _____ .

What Is The Church?

Called from the world—_____

Called together—_____

3. "Gates of Hell" the church is _____ , Satan is defending.

4. Why did Jesus use an imperfect Peter called "rock" (v. 18)?

   a. Rock is _____ . He is the foundation of the church (Ephesians 2:20).

   b. Rock is _____ -confession.

   c. Rock is _____ .

D. PETER REBUKED

"From that time Jesus began to show to His disciples that He must go to Jerusalem, and suffer many things from the elders and chief priests and scribes, and be killed, and be raised the third day. Then Peter took Him aside and began to rebuke Him, saying, 'Far be it from You, Lord; this shall not happen to You!' But He turned and said to Peter, 'Get behind Me, Satan! You are an offense to Me, for you are not mindful of the things of God, but the things of men'" (Matthew 16:21-23).

1. Jesus' death and resurrection shouldn't have _____ the disciples (v. 21).

2. You can quickly lose your _____ in God's plan (v. 23).

3. You can quickly go from "mindful of the Father's revelations," to "mindful of man's corrupt plans." Revealing Peter's _____ .

E. PETER THE ROCK—CRACKED

1. _____ . "One of the servant girls...noticed Peter warming himself by the fire...and said, 'You were one of those with Jesus of Nazareth.' But Peter denied, 'I don't know what you are talking about.'... 'This man is definitely one of them!' But Peter denied ... a little later...a bystander said, 'You must be one of them, because you are a Galilean' ... Peter cursed" (Mark 14:66-71, NLT).

2. Peter denied _____ times. Jesus asked him three times "Do you love (agape) Me?" Peter confessed, "Lord You know I love (phileo) You" (see John 21:15-17).

3. Jesus _____ His commission, "Then feed My sheep" (see John 21:17).

4. Jesus uses us when we come _____ to Him.

5. Mighty warriors for God can have _____ .

6. Your strength is not in your personality or your powerful will, it is in _____ .

7. What is the main lesson to learn from Peter?

Lesson 4:

ANSWER KEY

GIDEON

God Pushed An Introvert To Victory

A. WHEN GOD USES THE IMPERFECT: JUDGES 6:1-6

1. **Desert raiders**. The Midianties came, stole, and returned to the desert (Judges 6:2-3).

2. Israel hid in the **mountains**. "Gideon threshed wheat in the winepress, in order to hide it from the Midianites" (Judges 6:11).

3. Imperfect Gideon felt he was the bottom of the **totem pole**. "My family is the weakest in Manasseh, and I am the youngest in my father's house" (see 6:15).

B. GIDEON'S CALL: JUDGES 6:12-24

1. God **complimented** him. "The Lord is with you mighty warrior" (see v.12).

2. God **built him up**. "Go in the strength you have, and you will deliver Israel" (see v.14).

3. Gideon's first sign of imperfection. "Show me a sign" (see v. 17).

4. Gideon prepares a **sacrifice**, i.e., a goat, unleavened bread, and broth.

5. The Angel of the Lord, i.e., a **Christophany** disappeared in the smoke of the sacrifice. "You shall not die" (see v. 23).

C. THE FIRST CONFIRMATION FOR AN IMPERFECT PERSON: JUDGES 6:25-34

1. Challenge to get rid of an **altar to a foreign god**. "Tear down the altar of Baal that your father has, and cut down the wooden image" (v. 25).

2. Challenge your father's **unfaithfulness**. "That belongs to your father" (see v. 25).

3. Fearful Gideon did it at night. "But because he feared his father's household and the men of the city too much to do it by day, he did it by night" (v. 27).

4. A **life-threatening** leap of faith. "Bring out your son, he must die" (see v. 30).

5. Father's logic. "If Baal is a god, let him fight for himself" (v. 31, ELT). Gideon got a nickname, i.e., **Baal fighter**.

D. THE SECOND CONFIRMATION: JUDGES 6:36-40

1. Again, Gideon's **cowardly doubt**. "If You will save Israel by my hand" (v. 36).

2. **Natural**, wool attracts moisture.

3. **Unnatural**. Dew on sand and not on wool.

4. Principle of searching for God's will by a "fleece."

   a. God will not **reveal** His will by a "fleece."

   b. Do not make a choice based on a "fleece."

   c. However, a fleece **may confirm** what you already know.

   d. Do not put God **on the spot**, go by scripture.

   e. God leads by common sense, not by **luck**.

E. THE THIRD CONFIRMATION: JUDGES 7:1-6

1. Challenge the cowards to go home. "Whoever is fearful and trembling may turn back" (see 7:3). **22,000 left**.

2. Challenge the 10,000 to drink water.

   a. 9,700 "bowed down...to drink." Is this **idolatrous worship**?

   b. 300 "scooped water with the hand." They were **alert to the enemy**.

3. Why did God use only 300? "My grace is sufficient for you, for My strength is made perfect in weakness...that the power of Christ might rest upon me" (2 Corinthians 12:9). **Little is much when God is in it**.

F. THE FOURTH CONFIRMATION: JUDGES 7:7-15

1. Gideon still **doubted**. "Get up...if thou fear to go" (7:9-10, KJV).

2. Gideon will be encouraged. "Listen to what they say, then you will be strengthened" (see 7:11).

3. Gideon heard a dream of a loaf of barley bread tumbling on them. The name Gideon means "**cut barley**."

4. "When Gideon heard the dream and its interpretations, then he worshipped" (see v. 15). Gideon **finally understands**.

G. GIDEON DEFEATS THE ENEMY, I.E., 120,000,000: JUDGES 7:10-25

1. Strategy, 3 groups of 100 men each. **Faith-obedience** to divide his strength.

2. Swords stayed in sheaths, **trust was not in human ability**, trumpet in one hand and pitcher with torch in the other.

   a. Trumpet was God's call to **march**.

   b. Light is always God's **method**.

3. There's **power in words**, "The sword of the Lord and of Gideon" (vv. 18, 20).

4. There's **power in strategy**.

    a. Middle watch, **most fearful**.

    b. Enemy killed **one another in darkness**.

    c. Get help to **mop up**.

    d. Cut off retreat (v. 24).

H. PRINCIPLES FOR VICTORY

1. Our doubts and fears **holds us back**.

2. An imperfect person plus God makes a **confident warrior**.

3. An organized and obedient few can defeat a **multitude**.

4. God blesses when we **trust and obey**.

5. What is the main lesson to learn from Gideon?

GIDEON

God Pushed An Introvert To Victory

A. WHEN GOD USES THE IMPERFECT: JUDGES 6:1-6

1. _____ . The Midianties came, stole, and returned to the desert (Judges 6:2-3).

2. Israel hid in the _____ . "Gideon threshed wheat in the winepress, in order to hide it from the Midianites" (Judges 6:11).

3. Imperfect Gideon felt he was the bottom of the _____ . "My family is the weakest in Manasseh, and I am the youngest in my father's house" (see 6:15).

B. GIDEON'S CALL: JUDGES 6:12-24

1. God _____ him. "The Lord is with you mighty warrior" (see v. 12).

2. God _____ . "Go in the strength you have, and you will deliver Israel" (see v. 14).

3. Gideon's first sign of imperfection. "Show me a sign" (see v. 17).

4. Gideon prepares a _____ , i.e., a goat, unleavened bread, and broth.

5. The Angel of the Lord, i.e., a _____ disappeared in the smoke of the sacrifice. "You shall not die" (see v. 23).

C. THE FIRST CONFIRMATION FOR AN IMPERFECT PERSON: JUDGES 6:25-34

1. Challenge to get rid of an _____ . "Tear down the altar of Baal that your father has, and cut down the wooden image" (v. 25).

2. Challenge your father's _____ . "That belongs to your father" (see v. 25).

3. Fearful Gideon did it at night. "But because he feared his father's household and the men of the city too much to do it by day, he did it by night" (v. 27).

4. A _____ leap of faith. "Bring out your son, he must die" (see v. 30).

5. Father's logic. "If Baal is a god, let him fight for himself" (v. 31, ELT). Gideon got a nickname, i.e., _____ .

D. THE SECOND CONFIRMATION: JUDGES 6:36-40

1. Again, Gideon's _____ . "If You will save Israel by my hand" (v. 36).

2. _____ , wool attracts moisture.

3. _____ . Dew on sand and not on wool.

4. Principle of searching for God's will by a "fleece."

    a. God will not _____ His will by a "fleece."

    b. Do not make a choice based on a "fleece."

    c. However, a fleece _____ what you already know.

    d. Do not put God _____ , go by scripture.

    e. God leads by common sense, not by _____ .

E. THE THIRD CONFIRMATION: JUDGES 7:1-6

1. Challenge the cowards to go home. "Whoever is fearful and trembling may turn back" (see 7:3).
   _____ .

2. Challenge the 10,000 to drink water.

   a. 9,700 "bowed down...to drink." Is this _____ ?

   b. 300 "scooped water with the hand." They were _____ .

3. Why did God use only 300? "My grace is sufficient for you, for My strength is made perfect in weakness...that the power of Christ might rest upon me" (2 Corinthians 12:9).
   _____ .

F. THE FOURTH CONFIRMATION: JUDGES 7:7-15

1. Gideon still _____ . "Get up...if thou fear to go" (7:9-10, KJV).

2. Gideon will be encouraged. "Listen to what they say, then you will be strengthened" (see 7:11).

3. Gideon heard a dream of a loaf of barley bread tumbling on them. The name Gideon means
   "_____ ."

4. "When Gideon heard the dream and its interpretations, then he worshipped" (see v. 15).
   Gideon _____ .

G. GIDEON DEFEATS THE ENEMY, I.E., 120,000,000: JUDGES 7:10-25

1. Strategy, 3 groups of 100 men each. _____ to divide his strength.

2. Swords stayed in sheaths, _____ , trumpet in one hand and pitcher with torch in the other.

   a. Trumpet was God's call to _____ .

   b. Light is always God's _____ .

3. There's _____ , "The sword of the Lord and of Gideon" (vv. 18, 20).

4. There's _____ .

   a. Middle watch, _____ .

   b. Enemy killed _____ .

   c. Get help to _____ .

   d. Cut off retreat (v. 24).

H. PRINCIPLES FOR VICTORY

1. Our doubts and fears _____ .

2. An imperfect person plus God makes a _____ .

3. An organized and obedient few can defeat a _____ .

4. God blesses when we _____ .

5. What is the main lesson to learn from Gideon?

THOMAS
A Follower Of Jesus Doubted

A. WHO WAS THOMAS

1. Thomas was listed both 7th and 8th among disciples (Matthew 10:2-4; Mark 3:16-19; Luke 6:14-16).

THOMAS—THREE NICKNAMES

- Had a twin brother. *Didymas* means ditto, or duplicate, i.e., perhaps an __identical__ twin (John 20:24).

- Was from the tribe of Judah, or that was his father's name, i.e., *Judas, Thomas, Didymas.*

- Identified by his weakness, "*Thomas the doubter*"(see John 20:25).

2. First mention – first doubts. "Let us also go, that we may die with Him (Lazarus)" (John 11:16).

- What doubters do – they always see the __negative__, not the positive.

- Their first reaction is __pessimistic__.

- Are they __realist__?

- Who __taught them__ to be negative?

3. Second mention – __questioned__ Jesus' statement about heaven. "I go to prepare a place for you" (see John 14:3). Thomas replied, "No, we don't know...we have no idea where you are going" (John 14:5, NLT).

4. Third, Thomas' absence **speaks volumes**. On Sunday evening the day Jesus arose from the dead, Thomas was missing. "One of the twelve disciples, Thomas…was not with the others when Jesus came" (John 20:24, NLT).

   - Why – Thomas ran further away, because he doubted his future.

   - **Out of touch**, because he didn't want to be involved.

5. Fourth, **skeptical**. "I won't believe unless I see the nail wounds in His hands, put my fingers in them, and place my hand in His side" (John 20:25, NLT). A skeptic has made up their mind to not believe.

B. DOES DOUBT MAKE A PERSON IMPERFECT?

1. The day of resurrection ten disciples in Upper Room (John 20:19-24). "One of the twelve disciples, the twin, was not with them" (20:24).

2. Thomas was told by reliable witnesses, "We have seen the Lord" (John 26:24 NLT).

3. Disciples told Thomas their proof. "He (Jesus) showed them (ten disciples) His hands, and His side" (see John 20:20). Thomas could not believe them. A doubter makes decisions – not on **intellect or emotions** – but on their inner negative nature.

C. TWO WEEKS AFTER JESUS RESURRECTION

1. The next Sunday, Thomas was present. "Eight days later…Thomas was with them … Jesus was standing among them" (John 20:26, NLT).

2. Jesus knows our **unbelief and targets it**. "Put your finger … put your hand…don't be faithless…believe" (20:27, NLT).

3. Thomas makes highest expression of faith and loyalty. "My Lord and my God" (20:28). Identified using Old Testament expressions of faith: God = Elohim, i.e., creator, Lord = Jehovah, "the I am, I am."

D. TO TAKE AWAY

1. **Recognize** your doubts. "Lord, I believe; help thou mine unbelief" (Mark 9:24, KJV).

2. Pray for **faith** to overcome doubts. "Lord, increase our faith" (see Luke 17:5).

3. Listen to Jesus' promise to overcome **unbelief**. A father brought his needy son to Jesus saying, "If You can do anything...help us if you can" (see Mark 9:22). Jesus' response, "What do you mean, 'If I can'?" (Mark 9:23, NLT).

4. Follow Jesus' **instruction**. Jesus declared, "Anything is possible if a person believes" (Mark 9:23, NLT).

   - Faith is confidence and assurance about/from God (Hebrews 11:1).

   - Faith is a **gift** from God (Ephesians 2:8-9).

   - Only a **small amount** of faith is necessary (Luke 17:6)

   - Faith puts us in a right relationship to God (Romans 5:1).

   - Find faith in the **Word of God** (Romans 10:17).

   - Faith leads to obedience to God (Hebrews 11:7-12).

5. The real issue of faith is believing and acting what you know **about Jesus**. "Jesus was standing among them...he said to Thomas, 'Put your finger ... put you hand ... don't be faithless...believe'" (John 20:27, NLT).

6. Faith leads to correct understanding of Jesus. "My Lord and my God" (John 20:28). Thomas first acknowledged the **physical presence** of Jesus, then he acknowledged His deity, i.e., the **God-Man**.

Lesson 5:

QUESTIONS

THOMAS
A Follower Of Jesus Doubted

A. WHO WAS THOMAS

1. Thomas was listed both 7th and 8th among disciples (Matthew 10:2-4; Mark 3:16-19; Luke 6:14-16).

THOMAS—THREE NICKNAMES

- Had a twin brother. *Didymas* means ditto, or duplicate, i.e., perhaps an _____ twin (John 20:24).

- Was from the tribe of Judah, or that was his father's name, i.e., *Judas, Thomas, Didymas.*

- Identified by his weakness, "*Thomas the doubter*" (John 20:25).

2. First mention – first doubts. "Let us also go that we may die with him (Lazarus)" (John 11:16).

- What doubters do – they always see the _____ , not the positive.

- Their first reaction is _____ .

- Are they _____ ?

- Who _____ to be negative?

3. Second mention – _____ Jesus' statement about heaven. "I go to prepare a place for you" (see John 14:3). Thomas replied, "No, we don't know...we have no idea where you are going" (John 14:5, NLT).

4. Third, Thomas' absence _____ . On Sunday evening the day Jesus arose from the dead, Thomas was missing. "One of the twelve disciples, Thomas...was not with the others when Jesus came" (John 20:24, NLT).

    • Why – Thomas ran further away, because he doubted his future.

    • _____ , because he didn't want to be involved.

5. Fourth, _____ . "I won't believe unless I see the nail wounds in His hands, put my fingers in them, and place my hand in His side" (John 20:25, NLT). A skeptic has made up their mind to not believe.

B. DOES DOUBT MAKE A PERSON IMPERFECT?

1. The day of resurrection ten disciples in Upper Room (John 20:19-24). "One of the twelve disciples, was not with them" (20:24).

2. Thomas was told by reliable witnesses, "We have seen the Lord" (John 26:24).

3. Disciples told Thomas their proof. "He (Jesus) showed them (ten disciples) His hands, and His side" (see John 20:20). Thomas could not believe them. A doubter makes decisions – not on _____ – but on their inner negative nature.

C. TWO WEEKS AFTER JESUS RESURRECTION

1. The next Sunday, Thomas was present. "Eight days later...Thomas was with them ... Jesus was standing among them" (John 20:26, NLT).

2. Jesus knows our _____ . "Put your finger ... put your hand...don't be faithless...believe" (20:27, NLT).

3. Thomas makes highest expression of faith and loyalty. "My Lord and my God" (20:28). Identified using Old Testament expressions of faith: God = Elohim, i.e., creator, Lord = Jehovah, "the I am, I am."

D. TO TAKE AWAY

1. _____ your doubts. "Lord, I believe; help thou mine unbelief" (Mark 9:24, KJV).

2. Pray for _____ to overcome doubts. "Lord, increase our faith" (see Luke 17:5).

3. Listen to Jesus' promise to overcome _____ . A father brought his needy son to Jesus saying, "If You can do anything...help us if you can" (see Mark 9:22). Jesus' response, "What do you mean, 'If I can'?" (Mark 9:23, NLT).

4. Follow Jesus' _____ . Jesus declared, "Anything is possible if a person believes" (Mark 9:23, NLT).

   - Faith is confidence and assurance about/from God (Hebrews 11:1).

   - Faith is a _____ from God (Ephesians 2:8-9).

   - Only a _____ of faith is necessary (Luke 17:6)

   - Faith puts us in a right relationship to God (Romans 5:1).

   - Find faith in the _____ (Romans 10:17).

   - Faith leads to obedience to God (Hebrews 11:7-12).

5. The real issue of faith is believing and acting what you know _____ . "Jesus was standing among them...he said to Thomas, 'Put your finger ... put you hand ... don't be faithless...believe'" (John 20:26-27, NLT).

6. Faith leads to correct understanding of Jesus. "My Lord and my God" (John 20:28). Thomas first acknowledged the _____ of Jesus, then he acknowledged His deity, i.e., the _____ .

NAOMI

A Bitter Woman Who Lost Everything, Ended Up A Nourisher

A. HOW NAOMI COMPROMISED

1. She compromised her **spiritual priorities**.

    a. Did not continue in difficulties. "A famine in the land" (see Ruth 1:1).

    b. Enticed by the well-watered plains of Moab (1:1).

    c. Left the Promised Land. "Ephrathites of Bethlehem, Judah" (1:2).

2. She compromised her commitment **to the Lord**. When Ruth, her daughter-in-law wanted to go with Naomi, she directed Ruth to go back to her foreign god. "Look, your sister-in-law has gone back to her people and to her gods; return after your sister-in-law" (1:15).

3. Naomi compromised her **family influence**. Naomi's son, Chilion, married outside the faith (1:4).

4. Naomi ended up **bitter about** God's provision. "I went out full, and the Lord has brought me home again empty" (1:21). "Call me...Mara, for the Almighty has dealt very bitterly with me ..." (1:20).

B. WHAT NAOMI DID RIGHT

1. **Naomi recognized God's punishment.** Naomi recognized God's punishment. "The Lord has caused me to suffer and the Almighty has sent such tragedy" (1:21, NLT).

2. **Naomi's counsel toward family heritage.** When Ruth "happened" on Boaz's field, Naomi said, "'Blessed be he of the Lord, who has not forsaken His kindness to the living and the dead!' And Naomi said to her, 'This man is a relation of ours, one of our close relatives'" (2:20).

3. Naomi counseled toward **redemption**. "Then Naomi her mother-in-law said unto her, 'My daughter, shall I not seek security for you, that it may be well with you?'" (3:1).

4. Naomi counseled **patience and trust**. "Then she (Naomi) said, 'Sit still, my daughter . . . for the man will not rest until he has concluded the matter this day'" (3:18).

C. THE BLESSING OF NAOMI

"Then the women said to Naomi, 'Blessed be the Lord, who has not left you this day without a close relative; and may his name be famous in Israel! And may he be to you a restorer of life and a nourisher of your old age; for your daughter-in-law, who loves you, who is better to you than seven sons, has borne him'" (Ruth 4:14-15).

1. Naomi is given **more importance** in the Bible than Ruth.

   a. The women blessed Naomi (4:14).

   b. The child is recognized as "kin" to Naomi (4:14).

   c. Naomi had oversight for the child's care (4:16).

2. The child is **identified** with this grandmother (not father or grandfather). Note: legal line not through Naomi and Elimelech (4:21).

3. The child Obed would be **famous in Israel**.

   a. The word famous means, "name is proclaimed widely."

   b. Obed was the **great grandfather** of Daniel.

   c. Obed comes from two words, (1) Obadiah i.e., a **worshipper of God**, (2) *ebed*, i.e., **servant**. Obed was a true servant and worshipper of the Lord.

4. The child gave Grandmother Naomi a **purpose in life**.

   a. Naomi had been a **compromiser**, but she became a woman of **conviction**.

   b. Naomi didn't have **any hope**. She told Ruth, "Turn back, my daughters, go—for I am too old to have a husband. If I should say I have hope, if I should have a husband tonight and should also bear sons" (1:12). But God gave her a **new life**. "He (Obed) shall be unto thee, a restorer of thy life" (4:15, KJV).

   c. Naomi had no **spiritual energy**. "Call me Mara, for the Almighty hath dealt very bitterly with me" (1:20). But Obed **nourished** her old age. "And may he (Obed) be to you a restorer of life and a nourisher of your old age" (4:15).

5. Naomi gained **the love** of her daughter-in-law. "Then the women said to Naomi, 'Blessed be the Lord . . . your daughter-in-law, who loves you, who is better to you than seven sons" (4:14-15).

6. Naomi had the responsibility of **influencing** the child.

   a. Naomi was given a **second chance** to rear a son.

   b. A rich man like Boaz would need **a maid** for children, i.e., he got Naomi.

   c. "Then Naomi took the child and laid him on her bosom, and became a nurse to him" (4:16).

D. LESSONS TO TAKE AWAY

1. God can **overlook** the sins and mistakes of your youth and use you in your old age.

2. You can list Naomi's mistakes, but we remember how God used her **in spite of them**.

3. What is the main lesson to learn from Naomi?

Lesson 6:

NAOMI
A Bitter Woman Who Lost Everything, Ended Up A Nourisher

A. HOW NAOMI COMPROMISED

1. She compromised her _____ .

   a. Did not continue in difficulties. "A famine in the land" (see Ruth 1:1).

   b. Enticed by the well-watered plains of Moab (1:1).

   c. Left the Promised Land. "Ephrathites of Bethlehem, Judah" (1:2).

2. She compromised her commitment _____ . When Ruth, her daughter-in-law wanted to go with Naomi, she directed Ruth to go back to her foreign god. "Look, your sister-in-law has gone back to her people and to her gods; return after your sister-in-law" (1:15).

3. Naomi compromised her _____ . Naomi's son, Chilion, married outside the faith (1:4).

4. Naomi ended up _____ God's provision. "I went out full, and the Lord has brought me home again empty" (1:21). "Call me...Mara, for the Almighty has dealt very bitterly with me ..." (1:20).

B. WHAT NAOMI DID RIGHT

1. _____ . Naomi recognized God's punishment. "The Lord has caused me to suffer, and the Almighty has sent me such tragedy" (1:21, NLT).

2. _____ . When Ruth "happened" on Boaz's field, Naomi said, "'Blessed be he of the Lord, who has not forsaken His kindness to the living and the dead!' And Naomi said to her, 'This man is a relation of ours, one of our close relatives'" (2:20).

3. Naomi counseled toward _____ . "Then Naomi her mother-in- law said unto her, 'My daughter, shall I not seek security for you, that it may be well with you?'" (3:1).

4. Naomi counseled _____ . "Then she (Naomi) said, 'Sit still, my daughter . . . for the man will not rest until he has concluded the matter this day'" (3:18).

C. THE BLESSING OF NAOMI

"Then the women said to Naomi, 'Blessed be the Lord, who has not left you this day without a close relative; and may his name be famous in Israel! And may he be to you a restorer of life and a nourisher of your old age; for your daughter-in-law, who loves you, who is better to you than seven sons, has borne him'" (Ruth 4:14-15).

1. Naomi is given _____ in the Bible than Ruth.

   a. The women blessed Naomi (4:14).

   b. The child is recognized as "kin" to Naomi (4:14).

   c. Naomi had oversight for the child's care (4:16).

2. The child is _____ with this grandmother (not father or grandfather). Note: legal line not through Naomi and Elimelech (4:21).

3. The child Obed would be _____ .

   a. The word famous means, "name is proclaimed widely."

   b. Obed was the _____ of Daniel.

   c. Obed comes from two words, (1) Obadiah i.e., a _____ , (2) *ebed*, i.e., _____ . Obed was a true servant and worshipper of the Lord.

4. The child gave Grandmother Naomi a _____ .

   a. Naomi had been a _____ , but she became a woman of **conviction**.

   b. Naomi didn't have _____ . She told Ruth, "Turn back, my daughters, go—for I am too old to have a husband. If I should say I have hope, if I should have a husband tonight and should also bear sons" (1:12). But God gave her a _____ . "He (Obed) shall be unto thee, a restorer of life" (4:15, KJV).

   c. Naomi had no _____ . "Call me Mara, for the Almighty hath dealt very bitterly with me" (1:20). But Obed _____ her old age. "And may he (Obed) be to you a restorer of life and a nourisher of your old age" (4:15).

5. Naomi gained _____ of her daughter-in-law. "Then the women said to Naomi, 'Blessed be the Lord...your daughter-in-law, who loves you, who is better to you than seven sons" (4:14-15).

6. Naomi had the responsibility of _____ the child.

   a. Naomi was given a _____ to rear a son.

   b. A rich man like Boaz would need _____ for children, i.e., he got Naomi.

   c. "Then Naomi took the child and laid him on her bosom, and became a nurse to him" (4:16).

D. LESSONS TO TAKE AWAY

1. God can _____ the sins and mistakes of your youth and use you in your old age.

2. You can list Naomi's mistakes, but we remember how God used her _____ .

3. What is the main lesson to learn from Naomi?

SAMSON
Wrongly Trusted His Own Strength

A. THE BIRTH OF SAMSON

1. From the <u>weak unlikely tribe</u> "of the Danites" (Judges 13:2)

2. A Nazarite from birth (13:7), i.e., <u>separated to God</u>. (Numbers 6:1-13).

   a. Can't <u>cut hair</u>.

   b. Can't touch a <u>dead body</u>.

   c. Can't drink <u>wine</u> (fruit of the vine).

3. God's call. "He shall begin to deliver Israel ... Philistines" (13:5).

4. Samson's strength, <u>physical</u>, and the spirit of the Lord.

5. Samson's weakness, the flesh, i.e., <u>woman problem</u>.

6. "The Spirit of the Lord came mightily upon him" (see 14:6, 19; 15:4)

   a. Killed lion with <u>bare hands</u>.

   b. Killed 30 men for <u>clothes</u>.

   c. Killed Philistines, <u>hip and thigh</u> (15:8).

   d. Killed 1000 with <u>jawbone</u>.

   e. Destroyed temple and 3000 men.

B. DELILAH: JUDGES 16:4-21

1. **Fleshly attraction**. "Loved a woman" (16:4).

2. Delilah and lords knew Samson's weakness. "And the lords . . . said to her, 'entice him'" (16:5). **Enemy knows your weaknesses.**

3. Why? Her **love of money and his love of sex**.

4. First, bind me with green vines; second, bind me with new rope; third, bind my hair in loom.

5. Law of **gradual enticement**, slowly getting to the secret of his strength, slowly breaking down.

   a. **Resistance**.

   b. Self-imposed **road blocks**.

   c. **Fear** of danger.

6. Some are **tantalized** by sexual dangers.

7. Dangerous game these lovers play. She topped Samson's deception with her own deception.

8. God loves **symbols**; strength was not in hair, but in God. Hair was a symbol of strength.

9. Are you breaking God's symbols?

   a. God's house, i.e., attendance, baptism, etc.

   b. **Tithe**.

   c. Baptism.

   d. **Lord's Table**.

10. Samson was spiritually blinded before **physical blindness**. "Put out his eyes" (16:21).

    • Sin **binds** (v. 7, 11, 13).

    • Sin **blinds** (v. 21).

    • Sin **grinds** (v. 21).

C. SAMSON: THE ENIGMA

1. He lost God's presence. "He wist not that the Lord was departed from him" (16:20, KJV).

2. He allowed the world to rejoice in the **fall of God's man**. "When the people saw him (Samson) they praised their god" (v. 24, KJV).

3. He allowed world to make fun of fallen hero. "Call for Samson...he may make us sport" (v. 25, KJV).

4. His worst sin: self-indulgent **pleasure** that violated God's Word.

5. His worst pain: self-inflicted **punishment** that glorified the enemy.

6. His worst weakness: self-deceptive **ignorance** that leads away from his calling.

7. His greatest strength: not his physical power, but his faith in God in an age of national doubt and apostasy. "What shall I more say? Time would fail me to tell of . . . Samson . . . having obtained a good report through faith" (Hebrews 11:32, 39, KJV).

8. What is the main lesson to learn from Samson?

Lesson 7:

QUESTIONS

SAMSON

Wrongly Trusted His Own Strength

A. THE BIRTH OF SAMSON

1. From the _____ "of the Danites" (Judges 13:2)

2. A Nazarite from birth (13:7), i.e., _____ . (Numbers 6:1-13).

    a. Can't _____ .

    b. Can't touch a _____ .

    c. Can't drink _____ (fruit of the vine).

3. God's call. "He shall begin to deliver Israel . . . Philistines" (13:5).

4. Samson's strength, _____ , and the spirit of the Lord.

5. Samson's weakness, the flesh, i.e., _____ .

6. "The Spirit of the Lord came mightily upon him" (see 14:6, 19; 15:4)

    a. Killed lion with _____ .

    b. Killed 30 men for _____ .

    c. Killed Philistines, _____ (15:8).

    d. Killed 1000 with _____ .

    e. Destroyed temple and 3000 men.

B. DELILAH: JUDGES 16:4-21

1. _____ . "Loved a woman" (16:4).

2. Delilah and lords knew Samson's weakness. "And the lords . . . said to her, 'entice him'" (16:5). _____ .

3. Why? Her _____ .

4. First, bind me with green vines; second, bind me with new rope; third, bind my hair in loom.

5. Law of _____ , slowly getting to the secret of his strength, slowly breaking down.

    a.   _____ .

    b.   Self-imposed _____ .

    c.   _____ of danger.

6. Some are _____ by sexual dangers.

7. Dangerous game these lovers play. She topped Samson's deception with her own deception.

8. God loves _____ ; strength was not in hair, but in God. Hair was a symbol of strength.

9. Are you breaking God's symbols?

    a.   God's house, i.e., attendance, baptism, etc.

    b.   _____ .

    c.   Baptism.

    d.   _____ .

10. Samson was spiritually blinded before _____ . "Put out his eyes" (16:21).

    • Sin _____ (v. 7, 11, 13).

    • Sin _____ (v. 21).

    • Sin _____ (v. 21).

C. SAMSON: THE ENIGMA

1. He lost God's presence. "He wist not that the Lord was departed from him" (16:20, KJV).

2. He allowed the world to rejoice in the _____ . "When the people saw him (Samson) they praised their god" (v. 24, KJV).

3. He allowed world to make fun of fallen hero. "Call for Samson...he may make us sport" (v. 25, KJV).

4. His worst sin: self-indulgent _____ that violated God's Word.

5. His worst pain: self-inflicted _____ that glorified the enemy.

6. His worst weakness: self-deceptive _____ that leads away from his calling.

7. His greatest strength: not his physical power, but his faith in God in an age of national doubt and apostasy. "What shall I more say? Time would fail me to tell of . . . Samson . . . having obtained a good report through faith" (Hebrews 11:32, 39, KJV).

8. What is the main lesson to learn from Samson?

SOLOMON

The World's Wisest Made Bad Choices

A. SOLOMON

1. **Wisest**. God asked Solomon in a dream, "Ask, what I shall give you" (see 1 Kings 3:5). "All Israel saw that the wisdom of God was in him to do judgments" (see 1 Kings 3:28).

2. Queen of Sheba. "I believed not...until I came...behold, the half was not told me: thy wisdom and prosperity exccedeth the fame" (1 Kings 10:7).

3. Built **Solomon's Temple** for God's presence. It was one of the largest, most ornate temples and contained a complex of preparation rooms for thousands of worshippers. It was constructed from many resources, by thousands of workers, costing untold riches. "Solomon decided to build a temple to honor the name of God...70,000 laborers, 80,000 men to quarry stone, 3,600 foremen" (2 Chronicles 2:1-2, NLT).

4. Solomon wrote his principles for living: Proverbs – his **wisdom**, Song of Solomon – his **passion**, and Ecclesiastes – his **decline**.

5. Solomon ruled in **peace**. "Throughout the lifetime of Solomon, all of Judah and Israel lived in peace and safety; and each family had its own home and garden" (1 Kings 4:25, LB).

6. Solomon ruled an area larger than the **Holy Land**. "Israel and Judah were a wealthy, populous, contented nation at this time. King Solomon ruled the whole area from the Euphrates River...down to the borders of Egypt. The conquered peoples...sent taxes to Solomon and continued to serve him throughout his lifetime" (1 Kings 4:20-21, LB).

7. Improved standard of living **for all**. David's people were simple farmers. A yearly salary for a Levite minister was 10 shekels (Judges 17:10). Solomon paid a vineyard keeper 600 shekels (Song of Solomon 8:11).

8. Protected people by <u>forts, towers and armies</u>.

9. Solomon's <u>symbol</u> of power. "He also made a huge ivory throne and overlaid it with pure gold. It had six steps...there was no other throne in all the world so splendid" (1 Kings 10:18, 20, LB).

10. Solomon's <u>wealth</u>. "Each year Solomon received gold worth a quarter of a billion dollars" (1 Kings 10:14, LB). "All of King Solomon's cups were of solid gold...silver was not used because it wasn't considered to be of much value" (1 Kings 10:21, LB).

11. Solomon's <u>failure</u>, he didn't understand the real values in life. "I had greater possessions...I also gathered for myself silver and gold and the special treasures of kings and of the provinces. Then I looked on all the works that my hands had wrought...behold, all was vanity" (Ecclesiastes 2:7-8, 11).

12. His father David, pursued God through his <u>failures</u>. Solomon's successes pulled him from God. "His wives turned his heart after other gods ..." (1 Kings 11:4). "Solomon did evil in the sight of the Lord, and did not fully follow the Lord" (1 Kings 11:6).

B. LESSONS TO LEARN FROM SOLOMON

1. Just because God <u>used you</u> at a young age does not guarantee His usefulness in middle age or old age.

2. Be careful of the <u>good things</u> for which you pray, they could dilute your faith or take away your passion.

3. The most <u>valuable things</u> in life are not bought with money. "Wherever your treasure is, there the desires of your heart will also be" (Matthew 6:21, NLT). The desires of your heart are more important than your money. Your desires <u>reveal</u> who you are.

4. What is the main lesson to learn from Solomon?

Lesson 8:

SOLOMON
The World's Wisest Made Bad Choices

A. SOLOMON

1. _____ . God asked Solomon in a dream, "Ask, what I shall give you" (see 1 Kings 3:5). "All Israel saw that the wisdom of God was in him to do judgements" (1 Kings 3:16).

2. Queen of Sheba. "I believed not...until I came...behold, the half was not told me: thy wisdom and prosperity exccedeth the fame" (1 Kings 10:7).

3. Built _____ for God's presence. It was one of the largest, most ornate temples and contained a complex of preparation rooms for thousands of worshippers. It was constructed from many resources, by thousands of workers, costing untold riches. "Solomon decided to build a temple to honor the name of God...70,000 laborers, 80,000 men to quarry stone, 3,600 foremen" (2 Chronicles 2:1-2, NLT).

4. Solomon wrote his principles for living: Proverbs – his _____ , Song of Solomon – his _____ , and Ecclesiastes – his _____ .

5. Solomon ruled in _____ . "Throughout the lifetime of Solomon, all of Judah and Israel lived in peace and safety; and each family had its own home and garden" (1 Kings 4:25, LB).

6. Solomon ruled an area larger than the _____ . "Israel and Judah were a wealthy, populous, contented nation at this time. King Solomon ruled the whole area from the Euphrates River... down to the borders of Egypt. The conquered peoples...sent taxes to Solomon and continued to serve him throughout his lifetime" (1 Kings 4:20-21, LB).

7. Improved standard of living _____ . David's people were simple farmers. A yearly salary for a Levite minister was 10 shekels (Judges 17:10). Solomon paid a vineyard keeper 600 shekels (Song of Solomon 8:11).

8. Protected people by _____ .

9. Solomon's _____ of power. "He also made a huge ivory throne and overlaid it with pure gold. It had six steps...there was no other throne in all the world so splendid" (1 Kings 10:18, 20, LB).

10. Solomon's _____ . "Each year Solomon received gold worth a quarter of a billion dollars" (1 Kings 10:14, LB). "All of King Solomon's cups were of solid gold...silver was not used because it wasn't considered to be of much value" (1 Kings 10:21, LB).

11. Solomon's _____ , he didn't understand the real values in life. "I had greater possessions...I also gathered for myself silver and gold and the special treasures of kings and of the provinces. Then I looked on all the works that my hands had wrought...behold, all was vanity" (Ecclesiastes 2:7-8, 11).

12. His father David, pursued God through his _____ . Solomon's successes pulled him from God. "His wives turned his heart after other gods ..." (1 Kings 11:4). "Solomon did evil in the sight of the Lord, and did not fully follow the Lord" (1 Kings 11:6).

B. LESSONS TO LEARN FROM SOLOMON

1. Just because God _____ at a young age does not guarantee His usefulness in middle age or old age.

2. Be careful of the _____ for which you pray, they could dilute your faith or take away your passion.

3. The most _____ in life are not bought with money. "Wherever your treasure is, there the desires of your heart will also be" (Matthew 6:21, NLT). The desires of your heart are more important than your money. Your desires _____ who you are.

4. What is the main lesson to learn from Solomon?

RICH YOUNG RULER
A Wealthy Man Learned Value

A. THE RICH YOUNG RULER: LUKE 18:18-23

1. He came to the **right person**. "There came one running, and kneeled to him, and asked him, 'Good Master, what shall I do that I may inherit eternal life?'" (Mark 10:17, KJV).

2. He came with a right **attitude**. "Good Master" (v. 17).

3. He was **blameless**. Jesus answers...not commit adultery...not murder...not steal...not testify falsely... honor father and mother." The rich young ruler answered, "I've obeyed all these" (vv. 19-21).

4. His life was **money**. "One thing you haven't done...sell all...give all"(v. 22).

5. He never said "no" to Jesus with words. "He became sad, for he was very rich" (v. 23). The imperfection of **rejection**. "went away sad" (Mark 10:22).

6. The ultimate transforming action, "Jesus loved him" (Mark 10:21).

B. TRADITION SAYS THE YOUNG MAN WAS BARNABAS

1. His given name "Joseph" the one the apostles nicknamed Barnabas (Acts 4:16) which means *encourager*. He **motivated** by giving money. "He sold a field he owned and brought the money to the apostles" (see Acts 4:37).

2. Barnabas, a Levite, **illegally** owned property. "The Levites...will receive no allotment of land...they will have no land of their own" (Deuteronomy 18:1-2, NLT).

3. Barnabas obeyed Jesus because his wealth was **spiritually illegal**.

4. Barnabas was an apostle (Acts 14:14), but not one of the 12.

5. Barnabas encouraged Paul "When Saul arrived in Jerusalem, he tried to meet...all afraid of him... Barnabas brought him to the apostles" (Acts 9:26-27, NLT).

6. Church at Antioch sent money to Jerusalem church in drought. "Entrusting their gifts to Barnabas and Saul to take to the elders of the church in Jerusalem" (Acts 11:30, NLT).

7. Barnabas and Saul/Paul first missionaries (Acts 13:1-2).

8. Barnabas – the rich young ruler who originally left Jesus but came back to Jesus, wanted to take his nephew Mark on the second missionary journey, even though Mark had left them on the first trip (Acts 15:36-40).

   a. The imperfect Barnabas wanted to give a second chance to **imperfect Mark**.

   b. First trip John Mark left (13:13). Maybe because Paul took leadership away from his **uncle Barnabas**.

   c. Mark was son of Mary (Acts 12:12; Colossians 4:10).

   d. Many think **Mark** followed the Roman soldiers and Jesus on the night of His arrest. "One young man following behind was clothed only in a long linen shirt. When the mob tried to grab him, he slipped out of his shirt and ran away" (Mark 14:51-52, NLT).

C. LESSONS TO TAKE AWAY

1. Those who first turned away from Jesus can come back later and **serve successfully**.

2. Be like Jesus, love those who at first turn away, and **pray for them**.

3. One who tuned away can help **others** who turned away.

4. Be careful of those you criticize or disagree with; they may be a **future fellow worker**.

   a. "Paul disagreed strongly since John Mark had deserted them...had not continued with them in their work" (Acts 15:38, NLT).

   b. "We are sending another brother with Titus...he was appointed by the churches...as we took an offering to Jerusalem" (2 Corinthians 8:18-19, NLT).

5. None of us are **perfect workers**, praise God for using imperfect people.

6. What is the main lesson to learn from the Rich Young Ruler?

Lesson 9:

QUESTIONS

RICH YOUNG RULER
A Wealthy Man Learned Value

A. THE RICH YOUNG RULER: LUKE 18:18-23

1. He came to the _____ . "There came one running, and kneeled to him, and asked him, 'Good Master, what shall I do that I may inherit eternal life?'" (Mark 10:17, KJV).

2. He came with a right _____ . "Good Master" (v. 17).

3. He was _____ . Jesus answers...not commit adultery...not murder...not steal...not testify falsely...honor father and mother." The rich young ruler answered, "I've obeyed all these" (vv. 19-21).

4. His life was _____ . "One thing you haven't done...sell all...give all"(v. 22).

5. He never said "no" to Jesus with words. "He became sad, for he was very rich" (v. 23). The imperfection of _____ . "went away sad" (Mark 10:22).

6. The ultimate transforming action, "Jesus loved him" (Mark 10:21).

B. TRADITION SAYS THE YOUNG MAN WAS BARNABAS

1. His given name "Joseph" the one the apostles nicknamed Barnabas (Acts 4:16) which means *encourager*. He _____ by giving money. "He sold a field he owned and brought the money to the apostles" (see Acts 4:37).

2. Barnabas, a Levite, _____ owned property. "The Levites...will receive no allotment of land...they will have no land of their own" (Deuteronomy 18:1-2, NLT).

3. Barnabas obeyed Jesus because his wealth was _____ .

4. Barnabas was an apostle (Acts 14:14), but not one of the 12.

5. Barnabas encouraged Paul "When Saul arrived in Jerusalem, he tried to meet...all afraid of him... Barnabas brought him to the apostles" (Acts 9:26-27, NLT).

6. Church at Antioch sent money to Jerusalem church in drought. "Entrusting their gifts to Barnabas and Saul to take to the elders of the church in Jerusalem" (Acts 11:30, NLT).

7. Barnabas and Saul/Paul first missionaries (Acts 13:1-2).

8. Barnabas – the rich young ruler who originally left Jesus but came back to Jesus, wanted to take his nephew Mark on the second missionary journey, even though Mark had left them on the first trip (Acts 15:36-40).

   a. The imperfect Barnabas wanted to give a second chance to _____ .

   b. First trip John Mark left (13:13). Maybe because Paul took leadership away from his _____ .

   c. Mark was son of Mary (Acts 12:12; Colossians 4:10).

   d. Many think _____ followed the Roman soldiers and Jesus on the night of His arrest. "One young man following behind was clothed only in a long linen shirt. When the mob tried to grab him, he slipped out of his shirt and ran away" (Mark 14:51-52, NLT).

C. LESSONS TO TAKE AWAY

1. Those who first turned away from Jesus can come back later and _____ .

2. Be like Jesus, love those who at first turn away, and _____ .

3. One who tuned away can help _____ who turned away.

4. Be careful of those you criticize or disagree with; they may be a _____ .

   a. "Paul disagreed strongly since John Mark had deserted them...had not continued with them in the work" (Acts 15:38, NLT).

   b. "We are sending another brother with Titus...he was appointed by the churches...as we took an offering to Jerusalem" (2 Corinthians 8:18-19, NLT).

5. None of us are _____ , praise God for using imperfect people.

6. What is the main lesson to learn from the Rich Young Ruler?

SAUL/PAUL
The Consummate Legalist
Finally Gains Perfection

A. SAUL'S LAW KEEPING WAS IMPERFECT

1. He was a **flawed** law keeper (Philippians 3:4-6).

2. He **hated** Christ and persecuted Christians. "Saul was consenting to his (Stephen) death...great persecution against the church...went from house to house...throwing them into prison" (see Acts 8:1-2).

3. Saul's **rage**. "uttering threats with every breath...eager to kill the Lord's followers" (Acts 9:1, NLT).

4. The world's most perfect law keeper was **imperfect**.

5. Law keeping begins with a **head** issue, and following Christ begins with a **heart** issue.

B. SAUL (MEANS TO ASK) BECOMES PAUL (MEANS SMALL OR HUMBLE)

1. God let him almost reach **his goal**. "Went to high priest...requested letters...to Damascus...bring them bound to Jerusalem...almost to Damascus" (see Acts 9:1-3).

2. **Confrontation**. "Knocked to ground...loud voice...bright light...I am Jesus" (Acts 9:3-5, ELT).

3. Conversion when Saul recognized Jesus. "Called Him Lord" (v. 5).

4. Blind – both **spiritually** and physically. "He was blind...three days" (v. 9).

5. God told Ananias, "Saul is my chosen instrument to take my message to the Gentiles" (9:15, NLT). Ananias baptized Paul and he received his sight.

6. **Taught by God**. "I did not…consult with any human…nor apostles…went away into Arabia (desert)… three years…went to Jerusalem…saw only Peter…only other, James the Lord's brother" (see Galatians 1:15-18).

7. The *law man* **learned** *grace*. "God Himself revealed His mysterious plan to me…both Jews and Gentiles share equally…both belong to Christ Jesus" (see Ephesians 3:3-6).

C. LEARNING FROM PAUL

1. We have an **old nature**. "Your old sinful nature makes you want to sin" (Ephesians 4:22, ELT).

2. Our old nature **enslaves**. "I want to do what is good, but I don't. I don't want to do what is wrong, but I do it anyway" (Romans 7:19, NLT).

3. Our **new nature** – Christ in you – gives you power. "Put on your new nature" (Ephesians 4:24, NLT).

4. You were crucified and raised to new life **with Christ**. "My old self has been crucified with Christ… Christ lives in me" (Galatians 2:20, NLT). "Just as Christ was raised from the dead…we also live new lives in Him" (Romans 6:4, ELT).

5. Our new **passion** is Jesus. "For me, living means living for Christ" (Philippians 1:21, NLT).

6. Our new **power** is Jesus. "I can do everything through Christ who gives me strength" (Philippians 4:13, NLT).

D. WHY DOES GOD USE IMPERFECT PEOPLE?

1. Paul who thought he was perfect, was **unusable**.

2. Only when we see our imperfections as Jesus sees them, can we begin to be **used by Him**.

3. That means we must have greater faith, so we can accomplish greater things through the power of Christ.

4. After all, isn't it faith that makes us **acceptable** to Him and **useable** by Him?

5. The more we see our imperfection through the eyes of Jesus, the more we will trust in His forgiveness to accept us, and we will trust His power to use us.

6. Aren't you glad you are **imperfect**, so recognize it and let your **imperfections** be your starting place for God's usefulness.

7. What is the main lesson to learn from Paul?

Lesson 10:

QUESTIONS

SAUL/PAUL

The Consummate Legalist
Finally Gains Perfection

A. SAUL'S LAW KEEPING WAS IMPERFECT

1. He was a _____ law keeper (Philippians 3:4-6).

2. He _____ Christ and persecuted Christians. "Saul was consenting to his (Stephen) death...great persecution against the church...went from house to house...throwing them into prison" (see Acts 8:1-2).

3. Saul's _____ . "uttering threats with every breath...eager to kill the Lord's followers" (Acts 9:1, NLT).

4. The world's most perfect law keeper was _____ .

5. Law keeping begins with a _____ issue, and following Christ begins with a _____ issue.

B. SAUL (MEANS TO ASK) BECOMES PAUL (MEANS SMALL OR HUMBLE)

1. God let him almost reach _____ . "Went to high priest...requested letters...to Damascus...bring them bound to Jerusalem...almost to Damascus" (see Acts 9:1-3).

2. _____ . "Knocked to ground...loud voice...bright light...I am Jesus" (Acts 9:3-5, ELT).

3. Conversion when Saul recognized Jesus. "Called Him Lord" (v. 5).

4. Blind – both _____ and physically. "He was blind...three days" (v. 9).

5. God told Ananias, "Saul is my chosen instrument to take my message to the Gentiles" (9:15, NLT). Ananias baptized Paul and he received his sight.

6. _____ . "I did not...consult with any human .. nor apostles...went away into Arabia (desert)...three years...went to Jerusalem...saw only Peter...only other, James the Lord's brother" (Galatians 1:15-18).

7. The *law man* _____ *grace*. "God Himself revealed His mysterious plan to me...both Jews and Gentiles share equally...both belong to Christ Jesus" (Ephesians 3:6).

C. LEARNING FROM PAUL

1. We have an _____ . "Your old sinful nature makes you want to sin" (Ephesians 4:22, ELT).

2. Our old nature _____ . "I want to do what is good, but I don't. I don't want to do what is wrong, but I do it anyway" (Romans 7:19, NLT).

3. Our _____ – Christ in you – gives you power. "Put on your new nature" (Ephesians 4:24, NLT).

4. You were crucified and raised to new life _____ . "My old self has been crucified with Christ...Christ lives in me" (Galatians 2:20, NLT). "Just as Christ was raised from the dead...we also live new lives in Him" (Romans 6:4, ELT).

5. Our new _____ is Jesus. "For me, living means living for Christ" (Philippians 1:21, NLT).

6. Our new _____ is Jesus. "I can do everything through Christ who gives me strengthens" (Philippians 4:13, NLT).

D. WHY DOES GOD USE IMPERFECT PEOPLE?

1. Paul who thought he was perfect, was _____ .

2. Only when we see our imperfections as Jesus sees them, can we begin to be _____ .

3. That means we must have greater faith, so we can accomplish greater things through the power of Christ.

4. After all, isn't it faith that makes us _____ to Him and _____ by Him?

5. The more we see our imperfection through the eyes of Jesus, the more we will trust in His forgiveness to accept us, and we will trust His power to use us.

6. Aren't you glad you are _____ , so recognize it and let your _____ be your starting place for God's usefulness.

7. What is the main lesson to learn from Paul?

PART THREE

LEARNING FROM
GOD'S IMPERFECT PEOPLE

POWERPOINT GUIDE

**Learning From God's
Imperfect People**

By
Elmer Towns

Introduction

Why God Uses Imperfections

A. IMPERFECT PEOPLE?

1. Positive: We learn victory is possible when God gives weak people strength to succeed.

2. Negative: We learn what not to do.

TEN IMPERFECT PEOPLE

- Jacob: A liar and trickster changed by a dream
- Noah: After walking with God got drunk
- Peter: A granite rock who cracked
- Gideon: God pushed him to victory
- Thomas: A Jesus follower who doubted
- Naomi: A bitter woman constantly desiring better, ended up a nourisher
- Samson: wrongly trusted in his own strength
- Solomon: the world's wisest made bad choices
- Rich Young Ruler: A wealthy man learned value
- Saul/Paul: The consummate legalist finally gains perfection

3. We learn we have sinned. "For all have sinned and missed God's presence" (Romans 3:23).

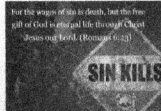

4. We learn we were blinded by our sin. "Satan, who is the god of this world, has blinded the minds of those who don't believe. They are unable to see the glorious light of the Good News. They don't understand this message about the glory of Christ, who is the exact likeness of God" (2 Corinthians 4:4, NLT).

5. We learn our good habits and deeds are worthless. "All have turned away; all have become useless. No one does good, not a single one" (Romans 3:12, NLT).

6. We are slaves to our old nature and sin. "I want to do what is good, but I don't. I don't want to do what is wrong, but I do it anyway. But if I do what I don't want to do, I am not really the one doing wrong; it is sin living in me that does it" (Romans 7:19-20).

B. THE BOOK OF JUDGES IS ABOUT WEAK LEADERS, i.e., IMPERFECT PEOPLE

"The Israelites did evil in the Lord's sight and served the images of Baal. They abandoned the Lord, the God of their ancestors, who had brought them out of Egypt. They went after other gods, worshiping the gods of the people around them. And they angered the Lord. They abandoned the Lord to serve Baal and the images of Ashtoreth" (Judges 2:11-13, NLT).

Things they did:

1. No belief. "Forsook the Lord" (2:12).

2. No obedience. "Turned quickly from the way" (2:17).

3. Did the opposite. "Served Baal and Ashtoreths" (2:13).

4. Flaunted evil. "Did evil in the sight of the Lord" (2:11).

C. WHY GOD USES IMPERFECT PEOPLE

1. For His glory. "Now all glory to God who is able to make you strong" (Romans 16:25, NLT).

2. As a testimony to the unsaved. "Remember ... few of you were wise in the world's eyes, or powerful, or wealthy ... instead God chose things the world considers foolish ... considered weak ... considered despised ... to bring to nothing what the world considers important ... so no one can ever boast in the presence of God" (1 Corinthians 1:26-29, NLT).

Slide 9 of 116

3. To demonstrate the power of God. "The message of the cross ... is the very power of God" (1 Corinthians 1:10, NLT).

WHY GOD USES IMPERFECT PEOPLE
- So, people will see God, not man
- So, people will worship God unreservedly
- So, people will be motivated to service
- So, Christ's body will work together
- Because God strategy uses imperfect people

Slide 10 of 116

D. WHAT IS THE PRINCIPLE?

1. Not I but Christ. Let Christ shine above your weaknesses. "I am crucified with Christ, nevertheless I live, yet not I, but Christ who dwells in me and the life which I live in the flesh I live by the faith of the son of God"(Galatians 2:20).

2. So, God's work is not done in a worldly way. "You don't see among yourselves many of the wise ... many of the ruling class ... many of the nobles ... who are called" (1 Corinthians 1:26, Phillips).

Slide 11 of 116

3. For God to work through us. "My strength (Christ) is made perfect in weakness" (2 Corinthians 12:9).

4. To manifest God's power. "My (Christ) power works best through weak people" (2 Corinthians 12:9, LB).

5. God calls a man/woman then does His work through them. "The Lord raised up a deliverer" (Judges 3:9).

6. To glorify God. "God has chosen the weak things ... that no flesh should glory in His presence" (1 Corinthians 1:28-29).

Slide 12 of 116

7. But don't stay "imperfect."

   a. Get a vision of what you can do.

   b. Find God's plan for your life (Jeremiah 29:11).

   c. Don't focus your life on your weaknesses.

   d. Work from your strength, that will lift your weaknesses. "I can do all things through Christ who strengthen me" (Philippians 4:13).

Slide 13 of 116

Lesson 1.

Jacob
A Liar And Trickster
Changed By A Dream

Slide 14 of 116

A. JACOB WAS PERFECTLY IMPERFECT

1. He enticed his brother Esau to sell his family birth right (Genesis 25: 26-34).

2. He deceived his father and lied to get the family's inheritance (Genesis 27:1-33).

3. Jacob had to run away from home. "Esau hated Jacob ... 'I will slay my brother'" (Genesis 27:41).

Slide 15 of 116

4. A dream from God changed his focus. "He dreamed ... a ladder ... the Lord stood above it ... the land whereupon you lie, to you will I give, and to thy seed" (Genesis 28:12-14).

   a. The land now has Jacob's new name – Israel.
   b. The people have Jacob's new name – the children of Israel.

Slide 16 of 116

5. Twenty years later, Jacob wrestles all night with a Christophany (the person of God). "When the man saw that he would not win the match, he touched Jacob's hip, and wrenched it out of its socket ... 'I will not let you go unless you bless me'" (Genesis 32;25-26, NLT).

6. Name changed from Jacob the <u>deceiver</u>, to Israel <u>prince with God</u>. "Thy name shall no more be called Jacob, but Israel: for as a prince thou hast power with God and with men, and hast prevailed'(Genesis 32:28).

Slide 17 of 116

B. WHY WAS JACOB IMPERFECT?

1. His mother Rebekah was <u>as deceptive</u> as Jacob (Genesis 27:5-10).

2. His father was old and invalid (27:1), did not influence Jacob.

3. He had no <u>role models</u> to do right.

Slide 19 of 116

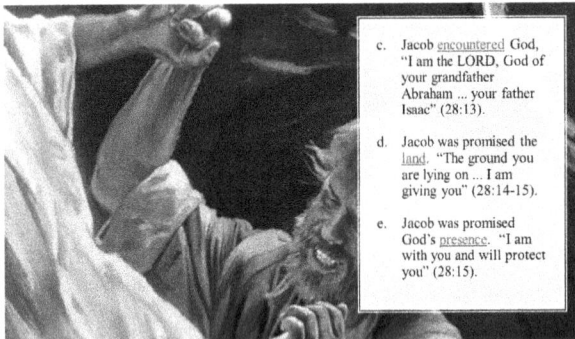

c. Jacob <u>encountered</u> God, "I am the LORD, God of your grandfather Abraham ... your father Isaac" (28:13).

d. Jacob was promised the <u>land</u>. "The ground you are lying on ... I am giving you" (28:14-15).

e. Jacob was promised God's <u>presence</u>. "I am with you and will protect you" (28:15).

Slide 21 of 116

3. Every imperfect believer needs:

a. A dream: (1) to be reminded <u>who you are</u>, (2) to keep your focus of <u>God's future</u>, (3) to <u>motive you and empower</u> you.

b. An encounter with God must demonstrate: (1) to show God your <u>determination</u> to serve Him, (2) to let <u>God</u> "touch" you, (3) to see <u>God's face</u>.

Slide 23 of 116

7. Even through a deceiver and imperfect, Jacob's <u>deep heart decision</u> was for God's blessing.

8. What can we learn? Deep passionate, sacrificial faith <u>pleases God</u> (Hebrews 11:6).

Slide 18 of 116

C. TO CHALLENGE AND CHANGE IMPERFECT PEOPLE

1. Jacob defined by a <u>dream</u> of a ladder and God at the top (Genesis 27:12-22).

a. Jacob left home in <u>obedience</u>. "Jacob obeyed his parents" (28:7).
b. Jacob was reminded by God to make a mighty nation of his children (28:2-4).

Slide 20 of 116

2. Jacob encountered God's presence twenty years later.

a. Threat from his <u>father-in-law</u>. "Laban caught ... Laban demanded ... Laban challenged, why did you deceive me" (31:25-27).

b. Threat from <u>brother</u>. "Esau came, and with him four hundred men" (33:1).

c. Threat from an <u>intruder</u>. Left Jacob all alone, and man came and wrestled with him until the dawn" (32:24, NLT). A Christophany an appearance of God. "Jacob named the place Penial, "face of God" "I have seen God face to face" (32:30, NLT).

Slide 22 of 116

Lesson 2

Noah
After Walking With
God Got Drunk

Slide 24 of 116

A. WHAT NOAH DID FOR GOD

1. Godly. What is known about Noah? "Noah was a just man and perfect … and Noah walked with God" (Genesis 6:9).

2. Warned of judgment. Why did Noah build an ark? "By faith Noah being divinely warned of things not yet seen moved with godly fear, prepared an ark … by which he condemned the world" (Hebrews 11:7).

3. Carpenter. What was Noah's occupation? "God said to Noah … make yourself an ark of gopher wood" (Genesis 6:14).

Slide 25 of 116

4. Preacher. How did Noah warn the world? "Noah … a preacher of righteousness" (2 Peter 2:5).

5. Drinking. What sins did Jesus mention that Noah preached against?" As the days of Noah were, so also will be the coming of the Son of Man … drinking … until the day Noah entered the ark" (Matthew 24:37-38).

6. Satan worship. What were other sins the people committed? (Genesis 6:1-13).

7. God called. When did Noah enter the ark? "The Lord said to Noah, 'Come thou and all thy house into the ark'" (Genesis 7:1). He was 600 years old (Genesis 8:13).

Slide 26 of 116

B. WHAT NOAH DID WRONG

"And Noah began to be a farmer, and he planted a vineyard. Then he drank of the wine and was drunk, and became uncovered in his tent. And Ham, the father of Canaan, saw the nakedness of his father, and told his two brothers outside. But Shem and Japheth took a garment, laid it on both their shoulders, and went backward and covered the nakedness of their father. Their faces were turned away, and they did not see their father's nakedness. So Noah awoke from his wine, and knew what his younger son had done to him. Then he said: 'Cursed be Canaan; a servant of servants He shall be to his brethren'" (Genesis 9:20-25).

Slide 27 of 116

1. A farmer. What was Noah's new occupation after the flood? "Noah began to be a husbandman, and planted a vineyard" (9:20).

2. What was Noah's threefold sin? "He (Noah) drank of the wine, and was drunken, and he was uncovered within the tent" (Genesis 9:21).
   a. Drunken. He preached against it.
   b. Exposure. He uncovered himself, i.e., gulah (reflective)
   c. Lack of role model.

Slide 28 of 116

3. How did Noah know? "Noah awoke from his wine, and knew what his younger son had done to him" (9:24).
   a. Special revelation.
   b. Inquiry. He asked or was told.
   c. Memory. A drunk man remembers some things.

Slide 29 of 116

C. WHAT WAS THE SIN OF HAM AND CANAAN?

Grandfather – Noah – sinned
Father – Ham – gossiped
Grandson – Canaan – laughed

Slide 30 of 116

1. Seeing only. "Ham, the father of Canaan saw the nakedness of his father, and told his two brethren" (Genesis 9:22). What went with seeing?
   a. Lust.
   b. Mockery.
   c. Rejection of father's authority to His God. (Morris)
   d. Not covering, i.e., showing disrespect.

2. Not seeing. "Shem and Japheth took a garment, and laid it upon their shoulders, and went backward, and covered the nakedness of their father; … and saw not their father's nakedness" (Genesis 9:23).

Slide 31 of 116

3. Why curse Canaan?
   a. Youngest. Ham was the youngest son of Noah, and Canaan youngest son of Ham (Genesis 10:6).
   b. Divine curse. This was not an "angry" grandfather. Since only God could know the future, Noah spoke by God's revelation. God cursed Canaan for what he did, and what He was to become.
   c. Noah recognized a rebellious attitude and perverse lust. Noah/God saw a weakness in Canaan and knew it would be perpetuated.
   d. Third generation always suffers the most, "cursed be Canaan, a servant of servants, shall he be to his brethren" (Genesis 9:25).

Slide 32 of 116

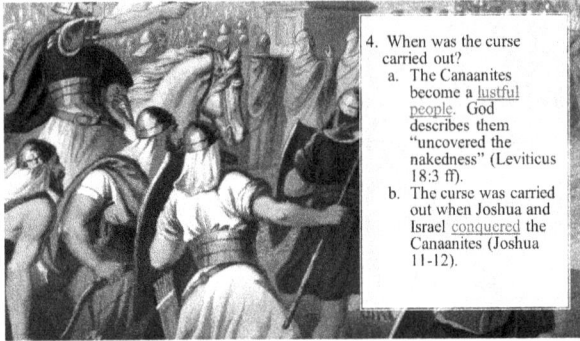

Slide 33 of 116

D. WHAT LESSONS CAN BE LEARNED ABOUT SINNING GRANDPARENTS

1. You never get too old to quit sinning.

2. You can fall at your greatest strength. "Let him that thinketh he standeth take heed lest he fall" (1 Corinthians 10:12).

3. Your fall can hurt your family. "Cursed be Canaan."

Slide 34 of 116

4. Your fall can come after God has greatly used you. Noah, Elijah, Peter, Paul, Uriah, David.

5. Just because you have done a lot for God, doesn't mean He will overlook your sin in old age.

6. The careless root of sin in a grandfather or father (lust or rebellion) can have disastrous results in grandchildren.

7. Drunkenness is not a private sin, nor is it something God overlooks.

Slide 35 of 116

8. The body is the temple of the Holy Spirit, and the child of God should be modest.
   a. Applies to all ages.
   b. Applies to sexual exposure.
   c. Applies to sexual viewing, i.e., lust.

Slide 36 of 116

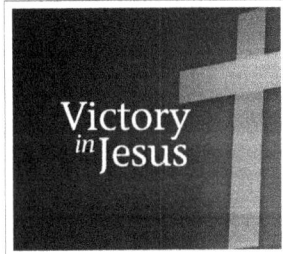

E. WHAT YOU NEED TO KNOW

1. God provides victory. "No temptation has overtaken you except such as is common to man; but God is faithful, who will not allow you to be tempted beyond what you are able, but with the temptation will also make the way of escape, that you may be able to bear it" (1 Corinthians 10:13).

Slide 37 of 116

2. God lives in your body. "He who commits sexual immorality, sins against his own body. Do you not know that your body is the temple of the Holy Spirit, who is in you … you are not your own" (1 Corinthians 6:18-19).

3. Old age sin will disqualify you. "But I discipline my body and bring it into subjection, lest, when I have preached to others, I myself should become disqualified" (1 Corinthians 9:27).

Slide 38 of 116

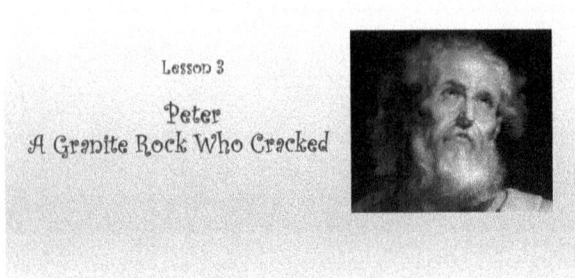

Slide 39 of 116

A. PETER THE ROCK

"When Jesus came into the region of Caesarea Philippi, He asked His disciples, saying, 'Who do men say that I, the Son of Man, am?' So they said, 'Some say John the Baptist, some Elijah, and others Jeremiah or one of the prophets.' He said to them, 'But who do you say that I am?' Simon Peter answered and said, 'You are the Christ, the Son of the living God.' Jesus answered and said to him, 'Blessed are you, Simon Bar-Jonah, for flesh and blood has not revealed this to you, but My Father who is in heaven. And I also say to you that you are Peter, and on this rock I will build My church, and the gates of Hades shall not prevail against it'" (Matthew 16:13-18, NKJV).

Slide 40 of 116

1. Jesus asked a question about His humanity. "Who do men say that I, the son of Man, am?"

2. The disciples answered:
   - John the Baptist – famous for preaching
   - Elijah – went to Heaven without dying
   - Jeremiah – to come before Messiah
   - One of the prophets – Moses (Deuteronomy 18:18)

Slide 41 of 116

3. Jesus asked a personal question. "But who do you say that I Am?" (v. 15).
   a. You must answer now.
   b. You will answer then. "Every tongue will confess" (Philippians 2:11).

Slide 42 of 116

B. THE "ROCK" CONFESSION BY PETER

1. The Christ means Messiah (Anointed), the coming Son of David to conquer Israel's enemies and rule on the throne. "The Son of the living God," Peter confessed Jesus' Deity.

2. Peter was called, Simon Bar-Jonah, i.e., "Son of Jonah" Peter's human heritage in contrast to Jesus' divine Sonship.

3. Jesus comments – humans didn't tell you this, My Father told you this (Revelation) (Matthew 16:17).

Slide 43 of 116

C. WHAT A ROCK PRODUCES

1. You are Peter (n) Petros = little loose stone. On this rock (f) Petra = ledge rock which is his confession.

2. "I will build My church" (v. 18).
   a. "I" – Jesus is the church planter.
   b. "Will" – Jesus will plant churches in the future.
   c. "Build" – Greek constant building.
   d. "My" – the church belongs to Jesus, not a pastor, deacons, or people.
   e. "Ecclesia" – the church is a group of out-called one.

Slide 44 of 116

What Is The Church?

Called from the world – separate
Called together – worship and serve

3. "Gates of Hell" the church is attacking, Satan is defending.

4. Why did Jesus use an imperfect Peter called "rock" (v. 18)?
   a. Rock is Jesus. He is the foundation of the church (Ephesians 2:20).
   b. Rock is message-confession.
   c. Rock is soul winner.

Slide 45 of 116

D. PETER REBUKED

"From that time Jesus began to show to His disciples that He must go to Jerusalem, and suffer many things from the elders and chief priests and scribes, and be killed, and be raised the third day. Then Peter took Him aside and began to rebuke Him, saying, 'Far be it from You, Lord; this shall not happen to You!' But He turned and said to Peter, 'Get behind Me, Satan! You are an offense to Me, for you are not mindful of the things of God, but the things of men'" (Matthew 16:21-23).

Slide 46 of 116

1. Jesus' death and resurrection shouldn't have surprised the disciples (v. 21).

2. You can quickly lose your usefulness in God's plan (v. 23).

3. You can quickly go from "mindful of the Father's revelations," to "mindful of man's corrupt plans." Revealing Peter's imperfection.

Slide 47 of 116

E. PETER THE ROCK – CRACKED

1. Denial. "One of the servant girls … noticed Peter warming himself by the fire … and said, 'You were one of those with Jesus of Nazareth.' But Peter denied, 'I don't know what you are talking about.'… 'This man is definitely one of them!' But Peter denied … a little later … a bystander said, 'You must be one of them, because you are a Galilean' … Peter cursed" (Mark 14:66-71, NLT).

2. Peter denied three times. Jesus asked him three times "Do you love (agape) Me?" Peter confessed, "Lord You know I love (phileo) You" (John 21:7, NLT).

Slide 48 of 116

3. Jesus re-instituted His commission, "Then feed My sheep" (John 21:7).

4. Jesus uses us when we come honestly to Him.

5. Mighty warriors for God can have feet of clay.

6. Your strength is not in your personality or your powerful will, it is in Christ.

7. What is the main lesson to learn from Peter?

Slide 49 of 116

Lesson 4

Gideon

God Pushed Him To Victory

Slide 50 of 116

A. WHEN GOD USES THE IMPERFECT: JUDGES 6:1-6

1. Desert raiders. The Midianties came – stole – and returned to the desert. (Judges 6:2-3).

2. Israel hid in the mountains. "Gideon threshed wheat in the winepress, in order to hide it from the Midianites" (Judges 6:11).

3. Imperfect Gideon felt he was the bottom of the Totem Pole. "My family is the weakest in Manasseh, and I am the youngest in my father's house" (6:15, CSB).

Slide 51 of 116

B. GIDEON'S CALL: JUDGES 6:12-24

1. God complimented him. "The Lord is with you mighty warrior" (v. 12, CSB).

2. God built him up. "Go in the strength you have, and you will deliver Israel" (v. 14, CSB).

3. Gideon's first sign of imperfection. "Show me a sign" (v. 17).

4. Gideon prepares a sacrifice, i.e., a goat, unleavened bread, and broth.

5. The Angel of the Lord, i.e., a Christophany disappeared in the smoke of the sacrifice. "You shall not die" (v. 23).

Slide 52 of 116

C. THE FIRST CONFIRMATION FOR AN IMPERFECT PERSON: JUDGES 6:25-34

1. Challenge to get rid of an altar to a foreign god. "Tear down the altar of Baal that your father has, and cut down the wooden image" (v. 25).

2. Challenge your father's unfaithfulness. "That belongs to your father" (v. 25).

Slide 53 of 116

3. Fearful Gideon did it at night. "But because he feared his father's household and the men of the city too much to do it by day, he did it by night" (v. 27).

4. A life-threatening leap of faith. "Bring out your son, he must die" (v. 27).

5. Father's logic. "If Baal is a god, let him fight for himself" (v. 31, ELT). Gideon got a nick name, i.e., Baal fighter.

Slide 54 of 116

D. THE SECOND CONFIRMATION: JUDGES 6:36-40

1. Again, Gideon's cowardly doubt. "If You will save Israel by my hand" (v. 36).

2. Natural, wool attracts moisture.

3. Unnatural. Dew on sand and not on wool.

Slide 55 of 116

4. Principle of searching for God's will by a "fleece."
   a. God will not reveal His will by a "fleece."
   b. Do not make a choice based on a "fleece."
   c. However, a fleece may confirm what you already know.
   d. Do not put God on the spot, go by Scripture.
   e. God leads by common sense, not by luck.

Gideons Fleece

Slide 56 of 116

E. THE THIRD CONFIRMATION: JUDGES 7:1-6

1. Challenge the cowards to go home. "Whoever is fearful and trembling may turn back" (7:3). 22,000 left.

2. Challenge the 10,000 to drink water.
   a. 9,700 "bowed down … to drink." Is this idolatrous worship?
   b. 300 "scooped water with the hand." They were alert to the enemy.

3. Why did God use only 300? "My grace is sufficient for you, for my strength is made perfect in weakness … that the power of Christ might rest upon me" (2 Corinthians 12:9). Little is much when God is in it.

Slide 57 of 116

F. THE FOURTH CONFIRMATION: JUDGES 7:7-15

1. Gideon still doubted. "Get up … if thou fear to go" (7:9-10).

2. Gideon will be encouraged. "Listen to what they say, then you will be strengthened" (7:11, CSB).

3. Gideon heard a dream of a loaf of barley bread tumbling on them. The name Gideon means "cut barley."

4. "When Gideon heard the dream and its interpretations, then he worshipped" (v. 15). Gideon finally understands.

Slide 58 of 116

G. GIDEON DEFEATS THE ENEMY, i.e., 120,000,000: JUDGES 7:10-25

1. Strategy, 3 groups of 100 men each. Faith-obedience to divide his strength.

2. Swords stayed in sheaths, trust was not in human ability, trumpet in one hand and pitcher with torch in the other.
   a. Trumpet was God's call to march.
   b. Light is always God's method.

Slide 59 of 116

3. There's power in words, "The sword of the Lord, and of Gideon" (vv. 18, 20).

4. There's power in strategy.
   a. Middle watch, most fearful.
   b. Enemy killed one another in darkness.
   c. Get help to mop up.
   d. Cut off retreat (v. 24).

Slide 60 of 116

H. PRINCIPLES FOR VICTORY

1. Our doubts and fears hold us back.

2. An imperfect person plus God makes a confident warrior.

3. An organized and obedient few can defeat a multitude.

4. God blesses when we trust and obey.

5. What is the main lesson to learn from Gideon?

Slide 61 of 116

Lesson 5

Thomas

A Jesus Follower Who Doubted

Slide 62 of 116

1. Thomas was listed both 7th and 8th among disciples (Matthew 10:2-4; Mark 3:16-19; Luke 6:14-16).

THOMAS – THREE NICKNAMES
- Had a twin brother. *Didymas* means ditto, or duplicate, i.e., perhaps an identical twin (John 20:24).
- Was from the tribe of Judah, or that was his father's name, i.e., *Judas, Thomas, Didymas*.
- Identified by his weakness, *"Thomas the doubter"* (John 20:25).

Slide 63 of 116

2. First mention – first doubts. "Let us also go that we may die with him (Lazarus)" (John 11:16).
   - What doubters do – they always see the negative, not the positive.
   - Their first reaction is pessimistic.
   - Are they realist?
   - Who taught them to be negative?

Slide 64 of 116

3. Second mention – <u>questioned</u> Jesus' statement about heaven. "I go to prepare a place for you" (John 14:3). Thomas replied, "No, we don't know … we have no idea where You are going" (John 14:5).

4. Third, Thomas' absence <u>speaks volumes</u>. On Sunday evening the day Jesus arose from the dead, Thomas was missing. "One of the twelve disciples, Thomas … was not with the others when Jesus came" (John 20:24, NLT).
   • Why – Thomas ran further away, because he doubted his future.
   • <u>Out of touch</u>, because he didn't want to be involved.

Slide 65 of 116

5. Fourth, <u>skeptical</u>. "I won't believe unless I see the nail wounds in His hands, put my fingers in them, and place my hand in His side (John 20:25, NLT). A skeptic has made up their mind to not believe.

Slide 66 of 116

B. DOES DOUBT MAKE A PERSON IMPERFECT?

1. The day of resurrection ten disciples in Upper Room (John 20:19-24). "One of the twelve disciples, Thomas, nickname; the twin, was not with them" (20:24).

2. Thomas was told by reliable witness, "They told him, we have seen the Lord" (John 26:24).

3. Disciples told Thomas their proof. "He (Jesus) showed them (10 disciples) His hands, and His side" (John 20:20, NLT). Thomas could not believe them. A doubter makes decisions – not on <u>intellect or emotions</u> – but on their inner negative nature.

Slide 67 of 116

C. TWO WEEKS AFTER JESUS RESURRECTION

1. The next Sunday, Thomas was present. "Eight days later … Thomas was with them ... Jesus was standing among them" (John 20:26).

2. Jesus knows our <u>unbelief and targets it</u>. "Put your finger ... put your hand … don't be faithless … believe" (20:27).

3. Thomas makes highest expression of faith and loyalty. "My Lord and my God" (20:28). Identified using Old Testament expressions of faith: God = Elohim, i.e., creator, Lord = Jehovah, "the I am, I am."

Slide 68 of 116

D. TO TAKE AWAY

1. <u>Recognize</u> your doubts. "Lord, I believe; help thou mine unbelief" (Mark 9;24).

2. Pray for <u>faith</u> to overcome doubts. "Lord, increase our faith" (Luke 17:5).

3. Listen to Jesus' promise to overcome <u>unbelief</u>. A father brought his needy son to Jesus saying, "If thou canst do anything … help us if you can" (Mark 9:22). Jesus' response, "What do you mean, if I can" (Mark 9:23, NLT).

Slide 69 of 116

4. Follow Jesus' <u>instruction</u>. Jesus declared, "Anything is possible if a person believes" (Mark 9:23).

   • Faith is confidence and assurance about/from God (Hebrews 11:1).
   • Faith is a <u>gift</u> from God (Ephesians 2:8-9).
   • Only a <u>small amount</u> of faith is necessary (Luke 17:6)
   • Faith puts us in a right relationship to God (Romans 5:1).
   • Find faith in the <u>Word of God</u> (Romans 10:17).
   • Faith leads to obedience to God (Hebrews 11:7-12).

Slide 70 of 116

5. The real issue of faith is believing and acting what you know <u>about Jesus</u>. "Jesus was standing among them … he said to Thomas, 'Put your finger ... put you hand ... don't be faithless … believe'" (John 20:27, NLT).

6. Faith leads to correct understanding of Jesus. "My Lord and my God" (John 20:28). Thomas first acknowledged the <u>physical presence</u> of Jesus, then he acknowledged His deity, i.e., the <u>God-Man</u>.

Slide 71 of 116

Lesson 6

Naomi

A Bitter Woman
Who Lost Everything
Ended Up A Nourisher

Slide 72 of 116

150   LEARNING FROM GOD'S IMPERFECT PEOPLE

A. HOW NAOMI COMPROMISED

1. She compromised her spiritual priorities.
   a. Did not continue in difficulties. "A famine in the land" (Ruth 1:1).
   b. Enticed by the well-watered plains of Moab (1:1).
   c. Left the Promised Land. "Ephrathites of Bethlehem, Judah" (1:2).

2. She compromised her commitment to the Lord. When Ruth, her daughter-in-law wanted to go with Naomi, she directed Ruth to go back to her foreign god. "Look, your sister-in-law has gone back to her people and to her gods; return after your sister-in-law" (1:15).

Slide 73 of 116

3. Naomi compromised her family influence. Naomi's son, Chilion, married outside the faith (1:4).

4. Naomi ended up bitter about God's provision. "I went out full, and the Lord has brought me home again empty" (1:21). "Call me ... Mara, for the Almighty has dealt very bitterly with me ..." (1:20).

Slide 74 of 116

B. WHAT NAOMI DID RIGHT

1. Naomi recognized God's punishment. Naomi recognized God's punishment. "The Lord hath caused me to suffer, and the Almighty has sent me such tragedy" (1:21, NLB).

2. Naomi's counsel toward family heritage. When Ruth "happened" on Boaz's field, Naomi said, "Blessed be he of the Lord, who has not forsaken His kindness to the living and the dead! And Naomi said to her, This man is a relation of ours, one of our close relatives" (2:20).

Slide 75 of 116

3. Naomi counseled toward redemption. "Then Naomi her mother-in-law said unto her, 'My daughter, shall I not seek security for you, that it may be well with you?'" (3:1).

4. Naomi counseled patience and trust. "Then she (Naomi) said, 'Sit still, my daughter ... for the man will not rest until he has concluded the matter this day'" (3:18).

Slide 76 of 116

C. THE BLESSING OF NAOMI

"Then the women said to Naomi, 'Blessed be the Lord, who has not left you this day without a close relative; and may his name be famous in Israel! And may he be to you a restorer of life and a nourisher of your old age; for your daughter-in-law, who loves you, who is better to you than seven sons, has borne him'" (Ruth 4:14-15).

Slide 77 of 116

1. Naomi is given more importance in the Bible than Ruth.
   a. The women blessed Naomi (4:14).
   b. The child is recognized as "kin" to Naomi (4:14).
   c. Naomi had oversight for the child's care (4:16).

2. The child is identified with this grandmother (not father or grandfather). Note: legal line not through Naomi and Elimelech (4:21).

Slide 78 of 116

3. The child Obed would be famous in Israel.
   a. The word famous means, "name is proclaimed widely."
   b. Obed was the great grandfather of Daniel.
   c. Obed comes from two words, (1) Obadiah i.e., a worshipper of God, (2) ebed, i.e., servant. Obed was a true servant and worshipper of the Lord.

Slide 79 of 116

4. The child gave Grandmother Naomi a purpose in life.
   a. Naomi had been a compromiser, but she became a woman of conviction.
   b. Naomi didn't have any hope. She told Ruth, "Turn back, my daughters, go-for I am too old to have a husband. If I should say I have hope, if I should have a husband tonight and should also bear sons" (1:12). But God gave her a new life, "He (Obed) shall be unto thee, a restorer of life" (4:15).
   c. Naomi had no spiritual energy. "Call me Mara, for the Almighty hath dealt very bitterly with me" (1:20). But Obed nourished her old age. "And may he (Obed) be to you a restorer of life and a nourisher of your old age" (4:15).

Slide 80 of 116

5. Naomi gained the love of her daughter-in-law. "Then the women said to Naomi, 'Blessed be the Lord . . . your daughter-in-law, who loves you, who is better to you than seven sons" (4:14-15).

6. Naomi had the responsibility of influencing the child.
   a. Naomi was given a second chance to rear a son.
   b. A rich man like Boaz would need a maid for children, i.e., he got Naomi.
   c. "Then Naomi took the child and laid him on her bosom, and became a nurse to him" (4:16).

D. LESSONS TO TAKE AWAY

1. God can overlook the sins and mistakes of your youth and use you in your old age.

2. You can list Naomi's mistakes, but we remember how God used her in spite of them.

3. What is the main lesson to learn from Naomi?

Lesson 7

Samson

Wrongly Trusted In His Own Strength

A. THE BIRTH OF SAMSON

1. From the weak unlikely tribe "of the Danites" (Judges 13:2).

2. A Nazarite from birth (13:7), i.e., separated to God. (Numbers 6:1-13).
   a. Can't cut hair.
   b. Can't touch a dead body.
   c. Can't drink wine (fruit of the vine).

3. God's call. "He shall begin to deliver Israel ... Philistines" (13:5).

4. Samson's strength, physical, and the spirit of the Lord.

5. Samson's weakness, the flesh, i.e., woman problem.

6. "The Spirit of the Lord came mightily upon him" (14:6, 19; 15:4)
   a. Killed lion with bare hands.
   b. Killed 30 men for clothes.
   c. Killed Philistines, hip and thigh (15:8).
   d. Killed 1000 with jawbone.
   e. Destroyed temple and 3000 men.

B. DELILAH: JUDGES 16:4-21

1. Fleshly attraction. "Loved a woman" (16:4).

2. Delilah and the lords knew Samson's weakness. "And the lords ... said to her, 'entice him'" (16:5). Enemy knows your weaknesses.

3. Why? Her love of money and his love of sex.

4. First, bind me with green vines; second, bind me with new rope; third, bind my hair in loom.

5. Law of gradual enticement, slowly getting to the secret of his strength, slowly breaking down.
   a. Resistance.
   b. Self-imposed roadblocks.
   c. Fear of danger.

6. Some are tantalized by sexual dangers.

7. Dangerous game these lovers play. She topped Samson's deception with her own deception.

8. God loves symbols; strength was not in hair, but in God. Hair was a symbol of strength.

9. Are you breaking God's symbols?
   a. God's house, i.e., attendance, baptism, etc.
   b. Tithe.
   c. Baptism.
   d. Lord's Table.

SAMSON

10. Samson was spiritually blinded before physical blindness. "Put out his eyes" (16:21).

- Sin binds (v. 7, 11, 13)
- Sin blinds (v. 21)
- Sin grinds (v. 21)

Slide 89 of 116

C. SAMSON: THE ENIGMA

1. He lost God's presence. "He wist not that the Lord was departed from him" (16:20).

2. He allowed the world to rejoice in the fall of God's man. "When the people saw him (Samson) they praised their god" (v. 24).

3. He allowed world to make fun of fallen hero. "Call for Samson … he may make us sport" (v. 25).

Slide 90 of 116

4. His worst sin: self-indulgent pleasure that violated God's Word.

5. His worst pain: self-inflicted punishment that glorified the enemy.

6. His worst weakness: self-deceptive ignorance that leads away from his calling.

7. His greatest strength: not his physical power, but his faith in God in an age of national doubt and apostasy. "What more shall I say? Time would fail me to tell of … Samson … having obtained a good report through faith" (Hebrews 11:32, 39).

8. What is the main lesson to learn from Samson?

Slide 91 of 116

Lesson 8

Solomon

The World's Wisest
Made Bad Choices

Slide 92 of 116

A. SOLOMON

1. Wisest. God asked Solomon in a dream, "Ask, what I shall give you" (1 Kings 3:5). "All Israel saw that the wisdom of God was in him to do judgements" (1 Kings 3:16).

2. Queen of Sheba. "I believed not … until I came and saw … behold half was not told me, thy wisdom and prosperity exceedeth your fame" (1 Kings 10:7).

Slide 93 of 116

3. Built Solomon's Temple for God's presence. It was one of the largest, most ornate temples and contained a complex of preparation rooms for thousands of worshippers. It was constructed from many resources, by thousands of workers, costing untold riches. "Solomon decided to build a temple to honor the name of God … 70,000 laborers, 80,000 men to quarry stone, 3,600 foremen" (2 Chronicles 2:1-2, NLT).

4. Solomon wrote his principles for living in: Proverbs – his wisdom, Song of Solomon – his passion, and Ecclesiastes – his decline.

Slide 94 of 116

5. Solomon ruled in peace. "Throughout the lifetime of Solomon, all of Judah and Israel lived in peace and safety; and each family had its own home and garden" (1 Kings 4:25, LB).

6. Solomon ruled an area larger than the Holy Land. "Israel and Judah were a wealthy, populous, contented nation at this time. King Solomon ruled the whole area from the Euphrates River … down to the borders of Egypt. The conquered peoples … sent taxes to Solomon and continued to serve him throughout his lifetime" (1 Kings 4:20-21, LB).

Slide 95 of 116

7. Improved standard of living for all. David's people were simple farmers. A yearly salary for a Levite minister was 10 shekels (Judges 17:10). Solomon paid a vineyard keeper 600 shekels (Song of Solomon 8:11).

8. Protected people by forts, towers and armies.

9. Solomon's symbol of power. "He also made a huge ivory throne and overlaid it with pure gold. It had six steps … there was no other throne in all the world so splendid" (1 Kings 10:18, 20, LB).

Slide 96 of 116

10. Solomon's wealth. "Each year Solomon received gold worth a quarter of a billion dollars" (1 Kings 10:14, LB). "All of King Solomon's cups were of solid gold ... silver was not used because it wasn't considered to be of much value" (1 Kings 10:21, LB).

11. Solomon's failure, he didn't understand the real values in life. "I had greater possessions ... I also gathered for myself silver and gold and the special treasures of kings and of the provinces. Then I looked on all the works that my hands had wrought ... behold, all was vanity" (Ecclesiastes 2:7-8, 11).

12. His father David, pursued God through his failures. Solomon's successes pulled him from God. "His wives turned his heart after other gods ..." (1 Kings 11:4). "Solomon did evil in the sight of the Lord, and did not fully follow the Lord" (1 Kings 11:6).

B. LESSONS TO LEARN FROM SOLOMON

1. Just because God used you at a young age does not guarantee His usefulness in middle age or old age.

2. Be careful of the good things for which you pray, they could dilute your faith or take away your passion.

3. The most valuable things in life are not bought with money. "Wherever your treasure is, there the desires of your heart will be also" (Matthew 6:21, NLT). The desires of your heart are more important than your money. Your desires reveal who you are.

4. What is the main lesson to learn from Solomon?

Lesson 9

Rich Young Ruler
A Wealthy Man Learned Value

A. THE RICH YOUNG RULER: LUKE 18:18-23

1. He came to the right person. "There came one running, and kneeled to him, and asked him, 'Good Master, what shall I do that I may inherit eternal life?'" (Mark 10:17).

2. He came with a right attitude. "Good Master" (v. 17).

3. He was blameless. Jesus answers ... not commit adultery ... not murder ... not steal ... not testify falsely ... honor father and mother." The rich young ruler answered, "I've obeyed all these" (vv. 19-21).

4. His life was money. "One thing you haven't done ... sell all ... give all"(v. 22).

5. He never said "no" to Jesus with words. "He became sad, for he was very rich" (v. 23). The imperfection of rejection. "went away sad" (Mark 10:22).

6. The ultimate transforming action, "Jesus loved him" (Mark 10:21).

B. TRADITION SAYS THE YOUNG MAN WAS BARNABAS

1. His given name "Joseph" the one the apostles nicknamed Barnabas" (Acts 4:16) which means encourager. He motivated by giving money. "He sold a field he owned and brought the money to the apostles" (4:37).

2. Barnabas, a Levite, illegally owned property. "The Levites ... will receive no allotment of land ... they will have no land of their own" (Deuteronomy 18:1-2, NLT).

3. Barnabas obeyed Jesus because his wealth was spiritually illegal.

4. Barnabas was an apostle (Acts 14:14), but not one of the 12.

5. Barnabas encouraged Paul "When Saul arrived in Jerusalem, he tried to meet ... all afraid of him ... Barnabas brought him to the apostles" (Acts 9:26-27).

6. Church at Antioch sent money to Jerusalem church in drought. "Entrusting their gifts to Barnabas and Saul to take to the elders of the church in Jerusalem" (Acts 11:30, NLT).

7. Barnabas and Saul/Paul first missionaries (Acts 13:1-2).

8. Barnabas – the rich young ruler who originally left Jesus, but came back to Jesus, wanted to take his nephew Mark on the second missionary journey, even though Mark had left them on the first trip (Acts 15:36-40).
   a. The imperfect Barnabas wanted to give a second chance to imperfect Mark.
   b. First trip John Mark left (13:13). Maybe because Paul took leadership away from his uncle Barnabas.
   c. Mark was son of Mary (Acts 12:12; Colossians 4:10).
   d. Many think Mark followed the Roman soldiers and Jesus on the night of His arrest. "One young man following behind was clothed only in a long linen shirt. When the mob tried to grab him, he slipped out of his shirt and ran away" (Mark 14:51-52, NLT).

Slide 105 of 116

C. LESSONS TO TAKE AWAY

1. Those who first turned away from Jesus can come back later and serve successfully.

2. Be like Jesus, love those who at first turn away, and pray for them.

3. One who tuned away can help others who turned away.

Slide 106 of 116

4. Be careful of those you criticize or disagree with; they may be a future fellow worker.
   a. "Paul disagreed strongly since John Mark had deserted them ... had not continued with them in the work" (Acts 15:38).
   b. "We are sending another brother with Titus ... he was appointed by the churches ... as we took an offering to Jerusalem" (2 Corinthians 8:18-19, NLT).

5. None of us are perfect workers, praise God for using imperfect people.

6. What is the main lesson to learn from the Rich Young Ruler?

Slide 107 of 116

Lesson 10

Saul/Paul

The Consummate Legalist
Finally Gains Perfection

Slide 108 of 116

A. SAUL'S LAW KEEPING WAS IMPERFECT

1. He was a flawed law keeper (Philippians 3:4-6).

2. He hated Christ and persecuted Christians. "Saul was consenting to his (Stephen) death ... great persecution against the church ... went from house to house ... throwing them into prison" (Acts 8:1-2).

Slide 109 of 116

3. Saul's rage. "Uttering threats with every breath ... eager to kill the Lord's followers" (Acts 9:1).

4. The world's most perfect law keeper was imperfect.

5. Law keeping begins with a head issue, and following Christ begins with a heart issue.

Slide 110 of 116

B. SAUL (MEANS TO ASK) BECOMES PAUL (MEANS SMALL OR HUMBLE)

1. God let him almost reach his goal. "Went to high priest ... requested letters ... to Damascus ... bring them bound to Jerusalem ... almost to Damascus" (Acts 9:1-3).

2. Confrontation. "Knocked to ground ... loud voice ... bright light ... I am Jesus" (Acts 9:3-5, ELT).

3. Conversion when Saul recognized Jesus. "Called Him Lord" (v. 5).

Slide 111 of 116

4. Blind – both spiritually and physically. "He was blind ... three days" (v. 9).

5. God told Ananias, "Saul is My chosen instrument to take My message to the Gentiles" (9:15, NLT). Ananias baptized Paul and he received his sight.

6. Taught by God. "I did not ... consult with any human .. nor apostles ... went away into Arabia (desert) ... three years ... went to Jerusalem ... saw only Peter ... only other, James the Lord's brother" (Galatians 1:15-18).

7. The law man learned grace. "God Himself revealed His mysterious plan to me ... both Jews and Gentiles share equally ... both belong to Christ Jesus" (Ephesians 3:6).

Slide 112 of 116

C. LEARNING FROM PAUL

1. We have an old nature. "Your old sinful nature makes you want to sin" (Ephesians 4:22, ELT).

2. Our old nature enslaves. "I want to do what is good, but I don't. I don't want to do what is wrong, but I do it anyway" (Romans 7:19, NLT).

3. Our new nature – Christ in you – gives you power. "Put on your new nature" (Ephesians 4:24, NLT).

Slide 113 of 116

4. You were crucified and raised to new life with Christ. "My old self has been crucified with Christ … Christ lives in me" (Galatians 2:20, NLT). "Just as Christ was raised from the dead … we also live new lives in Him" (Romans 6:4, ELT).

5. Our new passion is Jesus. "For me, living means living for Christ" (Philippians 1:21, NLT).

6. Our new power is Jesus. "I can do everything through Christ who gives me strengthens" (Philippians 4:13, NLT).

Slide 114 of 116

D. WHY DOES GOD USE IMPERFECT PEOPLE?

1. Paul who thought he was perfect, was unusable.

2. Only when we see our imperfections as Jesus sees them, can we begin to be used by Him.

3. That means we must have greater faith, so we can accomplish greater things through the power of Christ.

4. After all, isn't it faith that makes us acceptable to Him and useable by Him?

Slide 115 of 116

5. The more we see our imperfection through the eyes of Jesus, the more we will trust in His forgiveness to accept us, and we will trust His power to use us.

6. Aren't you glad you are imperfect, so recognize it and let your imperfections be your starting place for God's usefulness.

7. What is the main lesson to learn from Paul?

Slide 116 of 116

PART FOUR

LEARNING FROM
GOD'S IMPERFECT PEOPLE

FINAL THOUGHTS

Afterword

BEGIN WITH YOUR IMPERFECTIONS

TOO often we brag about our spiritual heroes for the good each has accomplished. When we brag on them, we focus on their victory and their obvious strength that made them a hero. Yes – each has a unique strength, but we forget each was also human and born from sinful parents. Each was imperfect.

God has always used imperfect people to accomplish His purpose on earth. Why? So, that credit and glory from the victory goes back to Him. When the world was threatened by satan and demonic abuse, God used an imperfect Noah to save his family and animals for the continuation of civilization, but afterwards he got drunk.

When the ancient world was given over to idolatry, God called on imperfect Abraham to become the father of the Jewish nation, but remember he lied on two occasions to the authorities about Sarah not being his wife.

When the world faced seven long years of famine and starvation, God gave imperfect Joseph a vison of the future and a plan to eventually feed the multitudes. But remember he originally got himself in trouble by bragging and boasting to his brothers. When God's people – the Hebrew people – where inhumanely persecuted in Egyptian slavery, God delivered them using imperfect Moses, who later would be punished for boasting he could bring water out of the rock.

God always uses imperfect men and women who step into an impossible situation to face insurmountable challenges, with terrifying consequences, with limited resources. Yet these imperfect people with faith in God and an anointing by God have always won a victory for God whether they were named Joshua, Gideon, Deborah, Samuel, Ruth, David, Elijah or Jeremiah. To that list could be added Timothy, and Barnabas. Don't forget imperfect Peter who once denied he knew the Lord and cursed, yet was used powerfully on the Day of Pentecost. And the once egotistical and legalist Saul/Paul was used of God, perhaps most powerfully of all.

The fact that God would use imperfect followers is a continuing demonstration of His grace and mercy. It challenges you to offer your imperfect abilities to God to be used by Him.

He does not use perfect people today because no perfect people are available – He will use anyone, even you.

So what can you learn from imperfect people? Just as God used imperfect people in this book and throughout the pages of Scriptures, Almighty God will again stoop to use imperfect people – even you – so go out and serve Him.

Conclusion

WHY AN IMPERFECT MAN WROTE THIS BOOK

I am the perfect person to write a book on imperfect people, because I know I am not perfect. If anything, knowing I am imperfect motivates me to improve in all the ways I serve the Lord. I will never be perfect, but I will try and keep trying until I go to be with the Lord.

I am not the brightest star in Christianity. In grades 1-12, I always was a "C" student, except in the 7th grade when my teacher Miss Logan motivated the socks off me—I made straight "As" in her class. As soon as I got permission, I moved from the back row to the front row. She assigned each class member to write a seven page term paper. I chose the Panama Canal. For the first time in my life, I read several books all the way through, reading everything I could about the Panama Canal. I began taking notes, and learned how to quote authorities to give my paper respectability.

I was only 12 years old, and yet I turned our old empty dilapidated garage into my private office. I built a desk out of scape wood and sat it in the middle of the floor. I could not write on the surface because the old rough wood was too uneven. I found an old linoleum rug from our kitchen, cut it to length, and sat on a barrel at my desk. My bookshelf was an old wooden apple crate that I nailed against the wall to hold my books on the Panama Canal. I don't remember how I wrote; except I poured my soul into that paper.

Two days after I turned it in, Miss Logan announced to the class I would be giving a report on the Panama Canal when we came back from recess.

Recess was my favorite time of the day, and I was usually the first out the door. This time I hung back, closed the door and went to work. And with white chalk, the only color we used in my day, I began drawing on three panels of blackboard, a massive scale of the Panama Canal from the Pacific to the Atlantic Ocean. It included locks, underground drainage pipes and mountains in the background. I finished just as everyone came back into the classroom.

"What is this?" Miss Logan asked.

"Panama Canal," I answered.

She told me to go ahead. I stood for around 15 minutes to explain to the class everything I learned about the Panama Canal, taking them on a journey from one ocean to the other. Then I sat down.

"Elmer ..." Miss Logan paused. "I have learned more about the Panama Canal from you than anyone else I my life."

"Aw-shucks" was all I could say.

That experience changed my life. In my subconscious I learned I could teach, and one day I would teach a lot more than just about the Panama Canal. Also I learned I could write, and one day I would write great things about more than the Panama Canal.

Next year I was promoted to the 8th grade, and promptly went to sit on the first seat right under Miss Grady's desk. When she caught me day dreaming. She yelled,

"You don't deserve to be in the front seat, go sit in the back of the room." I flunked all my courses in the 8th grade. I was the perfect imperfect student; I usually did what I wanted to do. When I wanted to do right, I made myself do it. When I didn't want to, I didn't.

This book is about how God uses imperfect people. I graduate number 254 out of a class of a little more than 500 students from Savannah High School, June 8, 1950. I was about as average as you could imagine. I never made the honor roll again after Miss Logan ... because I did not try.

On Memorial Day, 1943, I was 11 years old. Mother took us to clean up her family cemetery near Sardinia, South Carolina. We did not have electric lawn mowers in those days or electric trimmers. Before we began, mother stood me before the McFadden family history monument, a large granite stone about 10 feet tall. It had an engraved history of the McFaddens who pioneered and developed that area of South Carolina. It began with John McFadden who came to the United States in 1730, receiving one of the eight Land-grants from James the III, King of England, to colonize the United States. Then all the history of the McFaddens were listed on the granite stone right down to my grandfather. My mother turned and said to me,

"Elmer ... you have McFadden blood in your veins. These men did something great with their lives ... now make me proud of you ... do something great with your life."

As I stood in front of that stone she told stories of how they cleared the land of timber, dug out tree roots for farmland, planted crops to feed their families and began building their log cabins and began living. She told me stories of how John McFadden fought in the Revolutionary War, how Robert Eli McFadden, my great-grandfather fought in the Civil War as a Lieutenant, came home freed his five slave families, gave each of them an acre of ground and told them they could build their own houses from his trees and it would belong to them. Then he rehired them as share croppers. Some of the grandchildren of those families were still working on the McFadden farm when I was a boy in Sardinia, South Carolina.

That talk about McFadden greatness moved me. I took off my shirt, took the weed sling and began cutting the underbrush throughout the whole cemetery. Then I hauled them out to the roadway and burned them. Later when people at the local Presbyterian church told me that I did a great job, all I could say was,

"Aw-shucks, it was nothing."

Because of my mother, I learned to work to make money so I could to buy all the things I wanted. I learned that life is not a gift, it is challenge. I learned my life would be what I would make of it. When I became a Christian, I determined to make my life count for Jesus Christ, and to make Him Lord of everything.

Some people saw some promise in me. In mechanical drawing I drew an ultra-modern futuristic house. My mechanical drawing teacher submitted it to a contest, and I won a work-scholarship through the Branninger Organization (Savannah Machine and Foundry) to Gregoria Tech University in Atlanta, Georgia. Also, the editor of the Savannah Evening Press nominated me to receive a scholarship to the local college, today named Armstrong State Universtiy. My scholarship had a title something like "most likely to succeed."

Every summer my mother and I worked on my grandfather's farm because she was executor of his estate after he died without a will. We lived in South Carolina on his farm, and I did odd jobs around the farm. Each fall I got a paper route. The first year when I was around 11 years old I had about 100 customers, the following year I got a route of about 150 customers, the third year I got a route of about 250 customers, the next year I had a route of about 350 customers, but that was not enough to satisfy me. I got up early every morning at 4:00 am and delivered the Savannah Morning News, then went to high school, and came home to deliver another 350 papers. I spent most of my money on movies and snacks and always paid for my friends.

Then I met Jesus Christ as Savior. That changed everything. Because He transformed the inner Elmer Towns into a new man in Jesus Christ (2 Corinthians 5:17).

LESSONS TO TAKE AWAY

Every day I try to grow in knowledge of the Word of God. But the more Bible I learn, and the more insight I get, the more imperfect I feel my knowledge of Scriptures. I dedicate what I have learned to God and ask Him to use me in the best way possible. The more I learn, the more imperfect I feel my knowledge of Scriptures.

The same way with prayer. I began a daily prayer list in January 1951. I still have all those sheets of paper where I have written my prayer requests. I don't feel I am a greater prayer-warrior after all those years. I don't feel I get greater answers after all these years. I keep praying and God keeps answering some of my requests – but not all. I describe my prayer life as imperfect.

Again, I have the same feeling about my teaching/preaching. Do I do it better with age and experience? I can't say yes, nor will I say I have declined in my ability. I still love to teach and preach and I still feel God uses me. But I am an imperfect teacher/preacher. I have had great experiences of being used by God in my early ministry as well as my later ministry. One thing I know, I am still an imperfect teacher/preacher.

PART FIVE

LEARNING FROM
GOD'S IMPERFECT PEOPLE

ADDITIONAL RESOURCES

POWERPOINT SLIDES:

To purchase and download the Powerpoint Slides go to
https://www.norimediagroup.com/pages/elmer-towns

VIDEO:

To purchase available video by Dr. Towns go to
https://www.norimediagroup.com/pages/elmer-towns

ADD-ON CONTENT

To purchase additional products in this series go to
https://www.norimediagroup.com/pages/elmer-towns

RELATED BOOKS

My Name is the Holy Spirit: Discover Me through My Name
Available at https://www.norimediagroup.com/pages/elmer-towns

Check out
our **Destiny Image**
bestsellers page at
destinyimage.com/bestsellers

for cutting-edge,
prophetic messages
that will supernaturally
empower you and the
body of Christ.

In the Right Hands, This Book Will Change Lives!

Most of the people who need this message will not be looking for this book. To change their lives, you need to **put a copy of this book in their hands.**

Our ministry is constantly seeking methods to find the people who need this anointed message to change their lives. **Will you help us reach these people?**

Extend this ministry by sowing three, five, ten, or *even more* **books today and change people's lives for the better!** Your generosity will be part of catalyzing the Great Awakening that many have been prophesying and praying for.

From

ELMER L. TOWNS

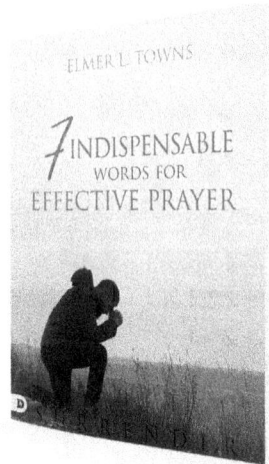

7 Indispensable Words for Effective Prayer

Prolific author, college and seminary professor, and co-founder of Liberty University, Elmer Towns has written a second Teaching Series consisting of six profound books designed to stir your spirit and increase your biblical knowledge: *Grandparents in the Bible; The Ten Commandments According to Jesus; 7 Indispensable Words for Effective Prayer; Habits of the Heart; When God Is Silent; What Is Right?* Intriguing titles with even more intriguing content.

7 Indispensable Words for Effective Prayer has been specially designed for maximum reading pleasure as well as study enjoyment. Supported with numerous relevant Scriptures throughout, this exploration on prayer and praying will undoubtedly make a significant impact on your daily interaction with your heavenly Father.

Purchase your copy wherever books are sold

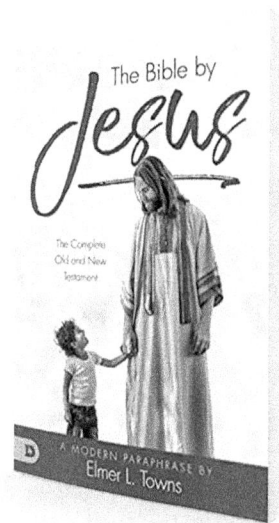

From

ELMER L. TOWNS

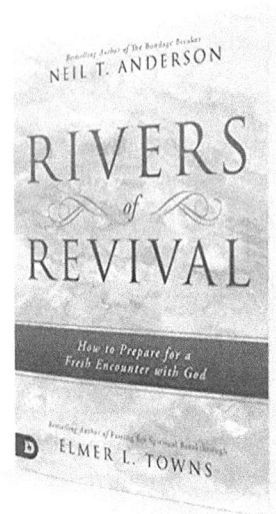

Since the Day of Pentecost, seasons of revival and awakening have brought refreshing to the spiritually dry, life to the spiritually dead, and miraculous encounters with the Holy Spirit.

In this timely and prophetic volume, two bestselling generals of the faith, Dr. Elmer Towns and Dr. Neil T. Anderson, offer collective wisdom, insight, and strategy on how you can experience and release a river of Holy Spirit outpouring into your world!

Additionally, Drs. Towns and Anderson have compiled contributions from other key authorities on revival who have encountered the move of God firsthand. Each contributor provides practical wisdom on how you can experience the Spirit's touch in your own life, church and even geographical region.

A fresh move of God is on the way. Prepare yourself to experience Holy Spirit outpouring like never before!

Purchase your copy wherever books are sold

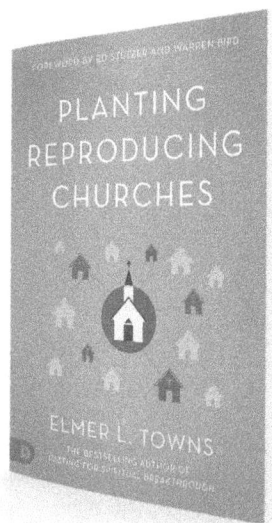

From

ELMER L. TOWNS

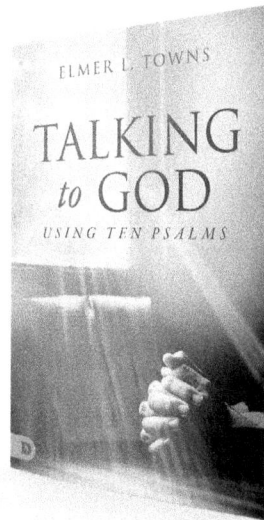

From

ELMER L. TOWNS

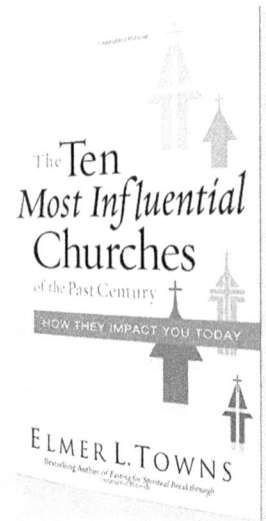

Your Church Can Influence the World

History has shown that great leaders have the ability to reach beyond the walls of their churches to influence cultures for Christ. We've seen it in the Pentecostal/Charismatic movement, in the explosive growth of house churches in Communist China, in the expansion of the Southern Baptist Convention, and in the world-wide rise of praise and worship music led by Hillsong Church, among other phenomena.

In *The Ten Most Influential Churches of the Past Century*, Dr. Elmer Towns presents evidence of the powerful influence of these churches and how their innovative strategies and faith accomplish these goals. Then he tells how you can apply these principles to your church. You will learn how some of the most influential leaders in Church history became conduits for your future ministry and how your church can experience exponential growth.

Most importantly, you will see that the great results in these ten churches grow out of the power of the Word of God, the ministry of many dedicated lay workers, the faith-producing ministry of great leaders—all under the anointing of the Holy Spirit.

Purchase your copy wherever books are sold

www.ingramcontent.com/pod-product-compliance
Lightning Source LLC
Chambersburg PA
CBHW062043090426

42740CB00016B/3004